The Wicked Wit of
CRICKET

The Wicked Wit of
CRICKET

MIKE HASKINS

MICHAEL O'MARA BOOKS LIMITED

First published in Great Britain in 2023 by
Michael O'Mara Books Limited
9 Lion Yard
Tremadoc Road
London SW4 7NQ

A CIP catalogue record for this book is available from the British
Library.

Papers used by Michael O'Mara Books Limited are natural,
recyclable products made from wood grown in sustainable forests.
The manufacturing processes conform to the environmental regulations
of the country of origin.

ISBN: 978-1- 78929-339-5 in hardback print format
ISBN: 978-1-78929-340-1 in ebook format

1 2 3 4 5 6 7 8 9 10
Cover and illustrations by Ian Baker
Designed and typeset by D23
Printed and bound by CPI Group (UK) Ltd, Croydon, CR0 4YY
www.mombooks.com

CONTENTS

INTRODUCTION

Cricket is one of the world's favourite sports. It is not only the national game of England but also that of Australia, Jamaica, Bermuda and Barbados, and – let's not forget – the Turks and Caicos Islands. Meanwhile, in India, Pakistan, Sri Lanka, Bangladesh and Afghanistan, it may not be the national game, but it is certainly the most popular!

The contest between leather and willow developed in England before being exported to all parts of the British empire and beyond. Having achieved independence, these countries today therefore use the great sport of cricket to assert their own national identities – preferably by thoroughly thrashing one another and, especially, the English.

Cricket is, as a result, a great and magnificent game enjoyed by millions around the globe. To many, the sport seems a sublime, almost religious experience. 'Cricket to us was more than play,' wrote the First World War poet

Edmund Blunden. 'It was a worship in the summer sun.' To Douglas Jardine, who captained England during the hugely controversial 'bodyline' tour, cricket was as 'battle and service and sport and art'. The playwright Harold Pinter went so far as to state: 'I tend to think that cricket is the greatest thing that God ever created on earth – certainly greater than sex, although sex isn't too bad either.'

Others have been rather more mystified by the game's attractions. The American actor and comedian Robin Williams described cricket as being like 'baseball on valium', while the playwright George Bernard Shaw commented: 'The English are not very spiritual people, so they invented cricket to give them some idea of eternity.'

This is, of course, all part of the attraction. Some might call it eternity; others might instead regard it as heaven. Whichever it may be, the world of cricket is one that is packed with larger-than-life characters, including the sport's great players past and present, legendary TV and radio commentators, unforgettable and often eccentric umpires, lyrical cricket writers and legions of enthusiastic and barmy fans.

What's more, if the evidence of their sayings or the many confrontations between them are anything to go by, many of these cricketing characters could have had second careers as comedians. Okay, some of them may have specialized in such areas of humour as the unintentional, the uncouth or the extremely childish. Nevertheless, these moments of hilarity have all contributed to the glorious history of one of the world's greatest sports.

So sit back and enjoy this sumptuous feast (or tea break) of the game's funniest stories from both on and off the field, together with a generous helping of quips, insults, pranks, mishaps, incredible facts, unforgettable characters, outrageous incidents and moments when words may not have come out quite as intended – all spread out across the clubhouse table in bite-sized pieces!

Whether you're a fan of Test Cricket, One Day Internationals, Twenty20, The Hundred, your national league, matches on the village green or just a knockabout out in the street, welcome to *The Wicked Wit of Cricket*.

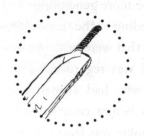

EARLY CENTURIES

Exactly when and where cricket first appeared is not clear. Some say an early reference to the game can be found in the wardrobe accounts of the Plantagenet King Edward I who ruled England from 1272 to 1307.

At six foot two, Edward I would surely have cut a fine figure as either a bowler or a batsman. And like so many great cricketers, Edward was known by a fun nickname: Longshanks. It was not Edward I who was supposedly a budding cricketer, however, but his young son, the future Edward II.

According to the wardrobe accounts, on 10 March 1301, John de Leek was repaid money that he had spent for the fifteen-year-old Prince Edward to play 'creag and other games' at Westminster and Newenden.

Some think that 'creag' may be an early reference to the game of cricket, while others think that 'creag' means nothing more than the terms 'crack' or 'craic'. In other words, Prince Edward was not playing cricket – he was just enjoying some more general fun or a bit of craic.

And after acceding to the throne himself, he went on to have fun in ways that were not approved of in the Middle Ages. Edward II was regarded by many as a weak and unpopular ruler who had allegedly scandalous relations with young men before coming to an unfortunate end when a red-hot poker was inserted into a part of his body where no one wants a red-hot poker. If it had been a red-hot cricket stump, presumably we'd have been told!

Before his unfortunate encounter with the poker, Edward II had been deposed in favour of his son Edward III who, in 1369, banned a game called *pila baculorea* or 'club ball', which seems to have been similar to cricket. Edward banned it because it was distracting his people from what he considered the more important business of the moment: waging war against France. In 1477, Edward IV banned a game referred to as 'Handyn and Handoute', which is believed to have been an early form of cricket. He was concerned his subjects were not doing enough archery practice and therefore anyone caught playing the game on his premises was subject to three years' imprisonment and a fine of £20. Anyone playing anywhere else got two years' imprisonment and a £10 fine.

Some argue that cricket may date back even further than the Edwards and that it in fact had its roots in a French game. A bat and ball game called *criquet* was introduced after the Norman Conquest. The words *wiket* meaning a small gate and *beil* meaning a crosspiece are also of Norman origin.

What can be said with a little more certainty is that cricket was being played some time before 1550 in areas of southern England, such as Kent, Sussex and Surrey. Other games involving batsmen, bowlers and fielders also existed but, unlike them, cricket had to be played on short grass, which was provided by forest clearings and land that had been used for sheep-grazing.

Some have narrowed down the area in which cricket was first played from Kent, Sussex and Surrey to a much more specific location: the Royal Grammar School, Guildford. At least one august and historic institution claims that the game of cricket was first invented and played here. And the august and historic institution that makes this claim is none other than the Royal Grammar School, Guildford. They even have a plaque on the wall to prove it. The story is backed up by a detail recorded in the Guildford court book from 17 March 1597. This describes a dispute over a plot of land, which provides the first universally accepted mention of cricket in English.

According to the court book, John Derrick, the fifty-nine-year-old coroner of Surrey, had been a pupil at the Royal Grammar School, where he and his friends had played cricket around the year 1550: 'Being a scholler in the ffree schoole of Guldeford hee and diverse of his fellows did runne and play at creckett and other plaies.'

The boys would not have had stumps but instead would have used a three-legged stool, such as might be used for milking or as an item of household furniture. And in other records from around the same time, this sort of stool is indeed referred to as a 'cricket' or perhaps 'cracket'.

The first reference to cricket being a game played by adults rather than children was in 1611. Two men were fined that year for breaking the Sabbath to play. Also in the same year, *A Dictionarie of the French and English Tongues* was published, which contains the earliest printed reference to cricket, which it defines as a boys' game. Even the eighteen-year-old Oliver Cromwell is said to have played cricket while he was training at the London Inns of Court in 1617.

A few years after the Lord Protector's death, Sir William Dugdale wrote that in his youth Cromwell had thrown 'himself into a dissolute and disorderly course'. He had become 'famous for football, cricket, cudgelling and wrestling', and even acquired 'the name of royster'.

It is claimed by some that cricket was banned when Cromwell became head of the English government, but in fact there is no evidence that cricket was specifically banned by the Puritan regime. Boys who were caught playing football on the Sabbath, on the other hand, could be whipped.

LET'S GO SLEDGING

Cricket has been established for over 500 years as a sport that provides drama, excitement and skill. Even better, it's also a great opportunity for hurling the most disgusting insults at your opponents.

The first use of the term 'sledging' is generally dated to the 1989 Ashes series when it was credited to Aussie bowler Carl Rackemann. His captain, Allan Border, was wondering what target to set for England on the final day's play at the Oval, London. Rackemann persuaded him to keep England on the field instead and thereby subject them to a prolonged period of mental and physical disintegration. Australia might not have enough time to get the ten wickets they needed but wearing the English team down helped ensure that they won the series.

In the years since, the term sledging has come to embrace the fine and delicate art of verbally winding up the opposition by means of wit and humour. Or, failing that, a barrage of insults, abuse, provocation and filthy language.

Australian fast-bowler Dennis Lillee had a line that he used on several batsmen through his career. 'I can see why you are batting so badly,' he would tell them. 'You've got a bit of shit on the end of your bat.'

The batsman would then check the end of his bat, only to hear Lillee's follow up line:

'Nah! Wrong end, mate!'

In a similar vein, when Robin Smith repeatedly found difficulty in returning Merv Hughes' deliveries, the master sledger called over to advise him: 'If you turn the bat over, you'll get the instructions, mate.'

The Zimbabwean bowler Eddo Brandes came out with one of cricket's most quoted lines when he faced Australia's Glenn McGrath. McGrath was becoming increasingly frustrated with Brandes just missing each ball.

In the end, McGrath had had enough. He went up to Brandes and asked him, 'Why are you so fat?'

'Because,' replied Brandes, 'every time I make love to your wife, she gives me a biscuit.' The Australian slip fielders were said to have succumbed to paroxysms of laughter in response.

The quote, however, seems to have been reported in several different forms over the years. Feel free, therefore, to replace the expression 'make love' with your own choice of terminology.

During the 1986–87 Ashes test, Australian wicketkeeper Rod Marsh welcomed Ian Botham to the crease by enquiring after his family.

'So how's your wife and my kids?' asked Marsh.

'The wife's fine,' replied Botham. 'The kids are retarded.'

In a similar vein, once during a match between Australia and the West Indies, Glenn McGrath put a question to the West Indies' Ramnaresh Sarwan.

'So,' asked McGrath, 'what does Brian Lara's dick taste like?'

'I don't know,' said Sarwan. 'Ask your wife.'

This rebound shot did not go down entirely well and McGrath exploded back: 'If you ever f***king mention my wife again, I'll f***ing rip your f***ing throat out.'

McGrath's outburst was understandable as his wife had been diagnosed with cancer. The Australians nevertheless recognized that Sarwan had not intended to be genuinely malicious.

South Africa were playing Australia. Batsman Daryll Cullinan took the crease against a slightly sturdy-looking Shane Warne. It was some years since the pair had last faced each other, so Warne called over: 'I've been waiting two years for another chance at you!'

'Looks like you spent it eating!' responded Cullinan.

Greg Thomas was bowling to Viv Richards in an English county match. After Richards had played and missed a few shots, Thomas told him: 'It's red, it's round. Now f***ing hit it!'

Richards then proceeded to thwack the next ball right out of the ground. Having done so, he turned and told Thomas: 'You know what it looks like! Now go and get it!'

James Ormond only played for England against Australia in one Test, in 2001. With England 300 behind, Ormond went out to bat, facing Steve Waugh's twin brother Mark.

'F*** me!' said Mark Waugh, greeting the slightly portly batsman. 'Look who it is! Mate, what are you doing out here? There's no way you're good enough to play for England!'

'Maybe not,' replied Ormond, 'but at least I'm the best player in my family.'

Another legendary verbal wind up occurred when New South Wales faced Victoria in a Sheffield Shield match.

Michael Slater took the crease to bat, only to hear bowler Shane Warne and wicketkeeper Darren Berry making a clock noise to each other:

'Tick.'

'Tock.'

'Tick.'

'Tock.'

'Tick.'

'Tock.'

'Tick.'

'Tock.'

This quickly became incredibly irritating, to the extent that Slater hit out and was caught at deep midwicket, at which point he heard a final sound-effect noise from Warne and Berry: 'Kaboom!'

On one occasion, word got out that Australia's Shane Watson had become concerned that the hotel in which his team was staying was haunted and as a result he had spent the night sleeping on his teammate Brett Lee's floor.

This was obviously too good an opportunity to miss, and Watson duly heard a ghostly cry from Darren Gough.

'Wooooooooh!' called Gough. 'Don't worry, Shane! You can sleep in my bed tonight!'

England bowler Monty Panesar, meanwhile, looked on the bright side of things when he said:

'Aussie sledging? I'm just glad they've heard of me!'

Merv Hughes became so synonymous with the art of sledging he was known as 'the greatest sledgend of all time'. Hughes has nevertheless wondered why he has been so associated with the practice.

'Why is that whenever the conversation turns towards sledging and insults in sports,' he asked, 'everyone in the room turns and looks at me? I didn't invent sledging and was certainly not the best at it. Perhaps I was more obvious because I had to do it from the middle of the pitch, seeing as I could not be bothered to run right to the batsman's end to deliver my insult *sotto voce*.'

Hughes did admit on another occasion: 'Sledging had always been a crucial part of my armoury. If you were facing me then you were the person I hated most in the whole world.'

Indeed, Hughes claimed that this use of 'verbal pressure' might have helped him claim a quarter of his 212 Test wickets. And, of course, over the years he became associated with some of the most classic and memorable lines that have defined the art of sledging.

One classic Merv Hughes line was to ask the player facing him: 'So … does your husband play cricket as well?'

In a slight variation when facing England's Graeme Hick, who was already struggling against the bowling onslaught, Hughes asked: 'What does your husband do when he is not watching you play cricket?' Hick was out the very next ball. Umpire Dickie Bird asked Hughes why he had been so aggressive towards Hick.

Hughes replied, 'He offended me in a former life.'

Michael Atherton claimed he had some difficulty understanding Merv Hughes' accent whenever the Aussie taunted him on the pitch. There was, though, at least one word he managed to pick up.

'I couldn't make out what he was saying,' said Atherton, 'except that every sledge ended with "arse-wipe".'

Hughes was, in Atherton's words, 'all bristle and bullshit', although off the pitch he found him 'extremely affable, in a cuddly toy sort of way'.

When Australia played the West Indies in the Caribbean, Hughes didn't say a word to Viv Richards. He simply stared at him after each delivery. In the end, it was Richards who broke the tense silence.

'This is my island, my culture,' said Richards. 'Don't you

be staring at me. In my culture, we just bowl.'

Hughes still didn't say anything. Instead, he waited until he had dismissed Richards before telling him: 'In my culture, we just say f*** off!'

When Pakistani batsman Javed Miandad faced Merv Hughes during a Test match in 1991, he called over to the Aussie bowler: 'Merv! You are a big, fat bus conductor!'

When Hughes managed to dismiss Miandad just a few balls later, he took delight in running past him while shouting: 'Tickets please!'

But sometimes words weren't enough even for the great Merv Hughes. Occasionally, he had to add sound effects.

When Viv Richards hit Hughes for four consecutive boundaries in one over, Hughes paused halfway down the pitch before producing a voluminous fart. After a brief pause, he challenged Richards: 'Let's see you hit that to the boundary!'

COMMENTARY BOX

Cricket coverage was first broadcast on BBC radio in 1927. There had, however, been broadcasts of cricket commentary in Australia as early as 1922. In 1938 at Lord's, the BBC broadcast the world's first television coverage of a Test match, and in 1957 the corporation's *Test Match Special* began broadcasting ball-by-ball radio coverage and continues to the present day. The world of cricket broadcasting has for almost 100 years, then, brought us a range of beloved characters and unforgettable moments. It's also delivered some extraordinary uses of language – some of it intentional.

One of the BBC's first and best remembered commentators was John Arlott. Rather than having been a professional cricketer, Arlott had in fact been a policeman in Hampshire. After making a radio address to King George VI on behalf of the police on VE Day in 1945, he began to appear more regularly on radio, eventually becoming one of the first commentators on *Test Match Special*. Arlott's commentaries were especially unforgettable for his one-liners.

He memorably once described Australian cricketer Ernie Toshack as batting 'like an old lady poking with her umbrella at a wasp's nest'. He commented more favourably when Clive Lloyd hit a four during a Test match in 1975, describing it as 'a stroke of a man knocking a thistle top with a walking stick'.

On another occasion, he described how Fred Trueman approached the wicket 'with the majestic rhythm that emerges as a surprise in the Spanish fighting bull' while another bowler's crouching run-up was 'like Groucho Marx chasing a pretty waitress'. And when South African bowler 'Tufty' Mann was causing problems for English batsman George Mann, Arlott's assessment was: 'What we have here is a clear case of Mann's inhumanity to Mann.'

The former England all-rounder Tony Greig became one of the game's great commentators. Nevertheless, there were moments when he got his words slightly mangled, such as his famous comment: 'In the back of Hughes' mind must be the thought that he will dance down the piss and mitch one.'

There were times when Greig also got the cricketers themselves mixed up, such as the occasion when he mistook Allan Border, who was on the field playing, with Rodney Marsh, who definitely was not: 'That was hit really hard by Rod Marsh ... no it wasn't, Rod Marsh has just walked into the dressing room. And, what's more – he's retired!'

There were also moments when Greig predicted what was about to happen only to have to contradict himself a split second later, for example when Steve Waugh dropped a dolly off Sachin Tendulkar: 'Straight up in the air ... Waugh won't drop this ... oh he's dropped it! I can't believe it! What's going on here?'

Or even more succinctly: 'What a magnificent shot! ... No, he's out.'

But, mostly, Greig was able to provide clear, unarguable insight into the game: 'Clearly the West Indies are going to play their normal game. Which is what they normally do.'

Brian Johnston – Johnners – was another of the commentary world's true greats. He began his career for the BBC with the Test match between England and India in 1946 and continued to work on TV and radio until he passed away aged eighty-one in January 1994. Even today, decades after his death, cricket fans in the UK and around the world will know many classic Johnston-isms off by heart. One reason for this, of course, is that he enjoyed nothing more than recounting his greatest and funniest moments whenever a chance arose!

Johnston recalled that he had once begun a broadcast on the BBC by saying, 'We welcome listeners with the news that Warr's declared.' He claimed that, shortly afterwards, an old lady phoned the BBC to ask, 'Against whom?'

On another occasion he said that a short time after his commentary that 'Ken Barrington was dropped when two', a woman wrote him a letter on the subject of carelessness by mothers.

There were, however, times when even Johnners got his words mangled, such as the unfortunate occasion when he attempted to refer to the unusual stance adopted by Hampshire's Harry Horton while batting.

Johnston intended to say, 'He looks like he's sitting on a shooting stick,' but managed to get the words 'shooting' and 'sitting' mixed up and thereby left listeners under the impression that Horton had been caught short on something called a 'sooting stick'.

Henry Blofeld is another much-loved commentator – notwithstanding the fact that Ian Fleming had been at school with his dad and purloined the family name for James Bond's arch nemesis.

Blofeld also occasionally got his words mixed up. In 1990, Graham Gooch achieved an epic 333 against India, the highest Test score ever made at Lord's. When he was finally dismissed, the crowd rose to give him a well-deserved ovation. After the cheering had died down slightly, Blofeld announced to the nation: 'I don't think I've ever heard a cloud crap like this one.'

Another BBC commentator also made an unfortunate

choice of words when a chance was missed off batsman Jack Crapp: 'It was an excellent performance in the field marred only when Harris dropped Crapp in the outfield.'

David Rayvern Allen's biography of John Arlott quotes the latter's famous enquiry to statistician and fellow member of the *Test Match Special* team Bill Frindall during the course of an Ashes test: 'What I really want to know, Bill, is if England bowl their overs at the same rate as Australia did, and Brearley and Boycott survive the opening spell, and there are not more than ten no-balls in the innings, and assuming that my car does 33.8 miles per gallon and my home is 67.3 miles from here – what time does my wife have to put the casserole in?'

Arlott also said of the *Test Match Special* statistician: 'Bill Frindall has done a bit of mental arithmetic with a calculator.'

By contrast, *TMS*'s longest serving contributor, Christopher Martin-Jenkins, did not seem to have need of such electronic assistance when he once commented: 'And we don't need a calculator to tell us that the run rate required is 4.5454 per over.'

Other correspondents have also had trouble with numbers over the years. South African broadcaster Michael Abrahamson once told the world: 'A very small crowd here today. I can count the people on one hand. Can't be more than thirty.'

TMS's **Don Mosey once noted: 'This is David Gower's hundredth Test, and I'll tell you something, he's reached his hundredth Test in fewer Tests than any other player.'**

In one legendary moment, the great BBC newsreader John Snagge announced: 'Yorkshire – 232 all out; Hutton ill … I'm sorry … Hutton – one hundred and eleven.'

It is not just numbers that can provoke confusion among cricketing pundits; basic geometry can also fox them.

Trevor Bailey, the former England all-rounder who appeared on *TMS* for twenty-seven years, once informed the listening audience: 'The Port Elizabeth ground is more of a circle than an oval. It is long and square.'

On another occasion, the Barbadian commentator Tony Cozier noted: 'The Queen's Park Oval – exactly as its name suggests. Absolutely round.'

The great Richie Benaud was not immune either. He once announced: 'Laird has been brought in to stand in the corner of the circle.'

The former Surrey and England cricketer Jim Laker summed up his national side's approach to the game. 'The aim of English cricket,' said Laker, 'is, in fact, mainly to beat Australia.'

During his career as a commentator Laker came out with a number of other great quotes, including: 'An interesting morning, full of interest,' 'And Ian Greig's on eight, including two fours,' and 'It's a unique occasion, really – a repeat of Melbourne 1977.'

Richie Benaud similarly failed to quite grasp the concept of uniqueness when he noted:

'This shirt is unique. There are only two-hundred of them.'

The issue of preparedness has also often been on the minds of cricket commentators. As Trevor Bailey once put it: 'I don't think he expected it. And that's what caught him unawares.'

Fred Trueman, on the other hand, once confidently asserted: 'Unless something happens that we can't predict, I don't think a lot will happen.'

Alan McGilvray, the former captain of New South Wales, whose commentating career spanned fifty years, once gave the following insightful assessment: 'This game will be over anytime from now.'

Tony Cozier once introduced Ian Botham with the words: 'Now Botham, with a chance to put everything that's gone before behind him.'

Don Mosey gave a cheerful assessment of matters when he said: 'Everyone is enjoying this except Vic Marks. And I think he's enjoying himself.'

The Sussex and England captain turned commentator Ted Dexter once asked: 'Who could forget Malcolm Devon?'

Presumably he had managed to temporarily forget Devon Malcolm's name.

At other times, the cricketing commentariat has been there to explain events on the pitch so we can all fully understand them. For example, Trevor Bailey's comments:

'Lloyd did what he achieved with that shot.'

'This series has been swings and pendulums all the way through.'

'The first time you face a googly you're going to be in trouble if you've never faced one before.'

'We owe some gratitude to Gatting and Lamb, who breathed some life into a corpse which had nearly expired.'

Christopher Martin-Jenkins once set the scene for listeners by saying: 'It's a perfect day here in Australia, glorious blue sunshine.'

While on one occasion Henry Blofeld helpfully put things into perspective: 'In the rear, the small, diminutive figure of Shoaib Mohammed, who can't be much taller than he is.'

Another time, Blofeld told the world: 'It's a catch he would have caught ninety-nine times out of a thousand.'

Richie Benaud once helpfully stated: 'His throw went absolutely nowhere near where it was going.'

And on another occasion Benaud told the world: 'That slow-motion replay doesn't show how fast the ball was travelling.'

In a similar vein, former Essex cricketer and Olympic fencer David Acfield commented: 'Strangely, in slow motion, the ball seemed to hang in the air for even longer.'

And in another classic moment of commentary, Brian Johnston announced: 'As he comes into bowl, Freddie Titmus has got two short legs, one of them square.'

Johnston claimed that afterwards a lady had written in to say there was no need to be so rude about peoples' disabilities.

Some commentators seem to have flirted with unfortunate anatomical analysis, such as Trevor Bailey: 'On the first day, Logie decided to chance his arm and it came off.'

Former West Indies fast bowler turned *TMS* commentator Colin Croft told listeners: 'The ball came back, literally cutting Graham Thorpe in half.'

Richie Benaud even seemed to suggest some sort of physical deformity when he described a moment of triumph on the pitch: 'There were congratulations and high sixes all round!'

One of the principal delights of cricket commentary is the opportunity for slightly smutty innuendo, whether accidental or, perhaps, sometimes intentional.

It is claimed that Richie Benaud on one occasion remarked: 'Steve Waugh is out injured with a badly swollen foot. But I saw him in the dressing room this morning and it didn't look like a foot to me. More like seven or eight inches.'

Another time, Benaud must have got some dirty guffaws when he said: 'He's usually a good puller – but he couldn't get it up that time.'

Christopher Martin-Jenkins, meanwhile, once commented: 'It is extremely cold here. The England fielders are keeping their hands in their pockets between balls.'

Trevor Bailey said, in reference to Peter Willey: 'I am, of course, a great Willey supporter.'

And Brian Johnston memorably relished the opportunities for double entendres. He once greeted radio listeners by saying: 'Welcome to Worcester, where you've just missed seeing Barry Richards hitting one of Basil d'Oliveira's balls clean out of the ground.'

Another time, Johnston informed the listenership: 'As you rejoin us at Leicester, Captain Ray Illingworth has just relieved himself at the pavilion end.'

At Lord's in 1969, the fast bowler Allan Ward of Derbyshire was playing in his first Test. One of Ward's ferocious deliveries bounced up and struck a painful blow to the box of New Zealand batsman Glenn Turner.

Turner dropped his bat and collapsed to the ground, where he spent several minutes writhing around in some discomfort. Male spectators at the ground and watching on television from around the world all collectively winced. Eventually, Turner managed to get back up on his feet, although still looking in some considerable pain. He was handed his bat back and prepared himself again at the wicket.

Brian Johnston commented: 'Very plucky. He's going on batting. One ball left!'

Rex Alston was a commentator for the BBC from the 1940s to the 1960s. At the end of a day's play at Lord's, Brian Johnston memorably passed the commentary over to Alston, who was covering a match at Edgbaston, by announcing, '... so over there for some more balls from Rex Alston.'

In 1962, Johnston spent some time helping Alston avoid mispronunciation of the Pakistani cricketer Afaq Hussein's name in case it ended up sounding a bit rude. Nevertheless, Alston then took to the airwaves to announce: 'A change of bowling – by Jove, we are to see Afaq to Knight at the Nursery End.'

Johnston was said to have been left giggling helplessly.

During a Test match at Headingley, while the Australians were fielding, the cameras decided to pan in to show the Aussie vice-captain Neil Harvey at leg slip. Johnston spoke later about how Harvey's image had suddenly filled the television screen. He had to think of something to say about him quickly before the picture changed. And so, Johnston heard the immortal words slipping from his lips: 'There's Neil Harvey, standing at slip, hands on knees, legs apart – waiting for a tickle.'

Johnston was once left in fits of giggles, with tears streaming down his face, when his fellow commentator Jonathan Agnew referred to England all-rounder Ian Botham being dismissed as a result of hitting his own wicket.

Agnew explained matters in all seriousness: 'Ian Botham was next to go. He got a short ball from Ambrose and just failed to get his leg over.'

Johnston tried to carry on but was eventually rendered incapable with laughter, only occasionally managing to beg his fellow commentator: 'Stop it, Aggers, please!'

Agnew recalled afterwards that Johnston had felt desperately concerned for having been responsible for the broadcast of such a vulgar and unprofessional moment. The next day, however, he was relieved to discover that the overwhelming response from the public was one of enjoyment at such an infectiously hilarious exchange.

Brian Johnston provided journalist Brian Viner with a recorded message for the answer machine on his home phone: 'And here we are at Lord's, with Brian Viner ninety-nine not out for England against Australia. It's been an absolutely marvellous innings ... and here comes Alderman from the Nursery End, lovely smooth action, he bowls, it's short-pitched, Viner hooks, he hasn't quite middled it, Border's running round from deep square ... and he takes a magnificent catch. It's very bad news for England, but Viner is out ... so at the tone please leave a message, and he'll get back to you.'

Johnston told the story of a man who had written to him asking what he should do after his pet Afghan hound had chewed up the insides of his copy of *Wisden*. Johnston said he made 'one or two rather wet suggestions, such as that he should build higher shelves or get a smaller dog'. He then realized that he should have just told the owner to have his dog's Wisden teeth taken out ...

The most famous of all Johnston-isms must be that which occurred in the course of his commentary during a 1976 match between England and the West Indies. He claimed that at the time he didn't realize what he had said until a lady wrote in to tell him that, while she enjoyed his commentaries, she felt that he should be more careful about how he phrased things.

Yes, this was the occasion when English batsman Peter Willey faced West Indian bowler Michael Holding at the Oval, thereby prompting Brian Johnston's legendary comment: 'The bowler's Holding; the batsman's Willey.'

There's just one problem. There is no record of the phrase having been used in a Test Match commentary in 1976 or indeed at any other point. It also seems that Willey did not face Holding at the time that Johnston claimed. Whatever the truth of the matter, it was clearly a great line, and one that Brian Johnston didn't want to waste!

SILLY BUGGERS MID-OFF

Some cricketers have become famed for their wit. Their elegant, brilliant and occasionally barbed bon mots have become as legendary as those of Oscar Wilde or Dorothy Parker. Other great players have instead favoured a different style of humour and have opted to relentlessly play the most childish pranks imaginable on one another.

In the late 1990s, Ricky Ponting began playing one-day international cricket for Australia under the captaincy of Steve Waugh. There was just one drawback as far as Ponting was concerned. While he enjoyed every minute on the pitch, in private he found Waugh to be 'pretty intense'. In particular, he discovered that when sitting next to his skipper on long plane journeys, there wasn't a great deal of conversation to be had. And so, during a twenty-hour flight to the UK for the 1999 World Cup, Ponting decided to play a little prank on the captain to try to break the ice.

Ponting boarded the plane, where he was delighted to receive a free toiletries bag, inside which he found shaving cream, a little toothbrush and all sorts of other fun-sized toiletry products. Waugh, meanwhile, had settled himself down next to Ponting, taken out his brand-new laptop and begun work on his tour diary.

Ponting pulled out the shaving cream canister from the goodie bag and gave it a shake. He told Waugh it was a great new brand of breath freshener. And then innocently asked if the skipper would like to try some.

Waugh took the canister, pointed the nozzle into his mouth and squirted it straight in. A moment later the Australian captain was coughing and spluttering and spitting soap froth all over his nice new laptop, which now presumably smelled slightly of sandalwood.

When Shane Warne was injured in 1996, Brad Hogg was selected for the Australian team as his replacement. Hogg, in his autobiography *The Wrong'Un*, recalled what happened when he joined the team for a one-day international tour in Sri Lanka.

Steve Waugh welcomed him to the side while team physio Errol Alcott gave out pills to the players ahead of their first match. Waugh proceeded to give the unsuspecting Hogg instructions as to how the tablets should be taken.

'Mate,' said Waugh, 'these pills are very important. You've got to take them. I'm going to go in and deal with it now.'

Hogg asked Waugh what he meant and Waugh went into a little more detail.

'You've got to put them up your anus, mate.'

This was all Hogg needed to hear. Without further ado, he excused himself, retired to the toilet and, as he put it, 'shoved them up my clacker'.

The ever-helpful Steve Waugh had given further instructions that the pills had to be put in 'really deep so they didn't come back out'. Again, Hogg saw no reason to question the medical advice that his teammate had so kindly provided.

'So that's what I did, getting the love finger right up there. What I didn't know is they were simple vitamin C tablets and of course they were meant to be taken the usual way. I felt uncomfortable for a few days, but I never got a cold.'

And hopefully they weren't effervescent vitamin C tablets, either – or the results could have been particularly distressing.

Ian Botham celebrated his birthday while he was on a tour of South Africa with David Gower. While staying at Leopard Hills Game Reserve, Gower helped prepare and source the ingredients for a lovely birthday cake for Botham. Gower recalled it was a beautifully iced chocolate cake, 'exactly the kind that Beefy likes'.

Botham was presented with the cake, festooned

with candles, and then encouraged to take a slice of this 'gorgeous confection'. He managed one mouthful before spitting it out with his eyes almost popping out of his head.

At this point, Botham was informed that the cake's mystery ingredient was not chocolate after all but a pile of fresh elephant dung that had been shovelled up that morning from a nearby road.

England endured a less than successful tour of Australia in 1990–91. A tour match against Queensland at the Carrara Oval on 21 January 1991, however, went better than the ongoing Test series. Unfortunately, this raised the spirits of David Gower and his teammate John Morris so much that they decided to perform an air display over the ground. They booked two Tiger Moth planes from an airfield nearby and flew low over the game while it was still ongoing.

The pair might have got away with the prank if it hadn't been for two things. A photographer covering the match recognized them through his telephoto lens and one of the pilots leaked the story to the press.

When Gower and Morris returned to the England dressing room, captain Graham Gooch asked, 'That wasn't you two up there by any chance, was it?'

Both Gower and his much less experienced and less well-paid teammate were fined the same amount of £1,000 and the incident seemed to hasten the end of Gower's Test career.

In July 2017, an excellent prank was played live on air on cricket legend Geoffrey Boycott during a broadcast of the BBC's *Test Match Special*.

Jonathan Agnew was commentating with Boycott on the final day of England's match against South Africa at the Oval when he produced a press release. Agnew proceeded to read out the statement, which he said had just been issued by the ICC.

'Further to the recent request from the South African government, the ICC has now considered the downgrading of all statistics, including runs and wickets, from the series played between England and the Rest of the World in 1970.

'The ICC agrees that the series was played against the spirit of the Gleneagles agreement and that in the interests of keeping cricket free from political interference, all matches will be removed from first-class records.'

'Well, I was not expecting that!' declared Agnew.

Boycott was not amused by the news and declared the decision to be 'a load of tripe!'

At this point, the *Test Match Special* statistician Andrew Samson reminded Boycott: 'You got a century in that series, didn't you? … That's going to be a bit of a problem if that's taken out.'

'Not really,' said Boycott.

But, as his *TMS* colleagues now went on to demonstrate, Boycott was wrong to dismiss the issue. Samson informed the increasingly rattled Yorkshireman of the ramifications of the ICC bombshell. The 151 centuries he had scored over his career would now be reduced to 150. Agnew mused further on the knock-on effects. Boycott's hundredth hundred had been at Headingley, his home ground.

'It was special,' said Agnew, before thinking for another moment and asking Samson, 'What date was Geoffrey's hundredth hundred?'

'The eleventh of August 1977,' came the reply. At the time, the fortieth anniversary of this great moment in Boycott's career was just a couple of weeks away.

Agnew turned to Boycott and asked: 'You haven't got anything planned for that?'

Boycott confirmed that he did indeed have something planned. He had arranged a charity fundraising event. One hundred and eighty guests had been invited to his house for the occasion.

'You'll have to cancel it,' Agnew told him solemnly. 'Actually, you invited me to that dinner. But you invited me under false pretences.'

'The way you're carrying on now, you're definitely not getting an invite,' Boycott told Agnew. 'I'm taking it back.'

He continued to react with alarm to the devastating news. 'We are not cancelling it. It's all sold and done,' he said, as the full tragedy of the situation sank in. 'It's a mess, isn't it? A complete mess!'

At which point, Agnew took pity and informed him: 'It's also a complete wind-up, Geoffrey!'

'Is that right?' exploded Boycott as laughter erupted around the commentary box. 'You muppet!'

In July 2020, Michael Atherton was commentating on the fourth day of England's first Test against the West Indies. During the afternoon, Atherton read out some messages live on air that celebrated the return of club cricket following that year's spring lockdown as a result of the Covid-19 pandemic. Among them was a mischievous tweet laced with double entendres from a Charlie Hilton, which read: 'Unbelievable scenes for Cockermouth Cricket Club, with Hugh Jardon bowling six for nine!'

Atherton duly announced to viewers around the world that 'Hugh Jardon' was 'six for nine at Cockermouth' before helpfully adding a connection to the batsman currently on screen: 'That's Ben Stokes' old club!'

By this time, Atherton's fellow commentators had, unlike the former England captain, realized that 'Hugh Jardon' was possibly not a genuine cricketer.

Simon Katich was on Australia's one-day tour of Sri Lanka in 2004 when his teammates decided to prank him.

While the team were staying at a hotel in the city of Dambulla, they noticed that there were monkeys living around the building. The hotel management had given strict instructions that residents should not feed the animals in order to try to keep them away from the premises. So Katich's teammates naturally decided to feed the monkeys to tempt them into the premises and up to Katich's room.

'They found some sugar cubes,' Katich recalled, 'and

they decided to pop them outside my door. Then what they do is they ring my room up and … pretend to be the housekeeping lady or whoever it was. So I'd answer the door and then, to my surprise, there's this monkey ready to jump in the room.

'Needless to say, I nearly jumped through the roof when I opened the door and there're a couple of monkeys trying to: one, get the sugar cubes, and then, two, jump into my room and ransack it.'

Katich found a number of his teammates giggling in their rooms along the hall but never succeeded in finding those directly responsible. It is, nevertheless, probably safe to assume that more than one cheeky monkey was involved in the prank.

Dickie Bird was umpiring a match between Northamptonshire and Lancashire at Old Trafford when he found himself locked inside his dressing room with smoke coming in under the door. Luckily, the fire was a very small one, which had been set by Allan Lamb and his Northants teammates.

Later, Lamb apologized to Dickie for his childish behaviour and the two men shook hands. Dickie then walked outside to drive home only to find Lamby had removed all the wheels from his car and left it propped up on bricks.

He had also left a nice note on the windscreen that read: 'Have a safe journey, Dickie!'

According to a story told by Henry Blofeld, Walter Robins, the captain of Middlesex at various times either side of the Second World War, had a habit when he was batting against a spin bowler. Robins would charge down the wicket towards the spinner but if it turned out that he missed the ball, he would simply carry on walking across the pitch to the pavilion without looking back.

Once, when he and his teammate Patsy Hendren were in to bat, however, Hendren decided to play a little joke on the captain just as he made his walk to the pavilion.

Robins had once again rushed out towards the bowler and missed the ball. He therefore continued walking without a backwards glance, but on this occasion he heard Hendren suddenly cry out after him: 'Look out! He's missed it!'

Hearing this, Robins spun round and threw himself down on the muddy pitch in a desperate attempt to get his bat back inside the crease.

When he picked himself up, he saw that the wicket was broken after all and the keeper was having a leisurely chat with first slip while tossing the ball from hand to hand.

In 1984, Australia were touring the West Indies. One day batsman Dean Jones arrived to join his teammates at the beach, where he found them up to their necks in the water throwing a cricket ball to one another.

Jones decided to dive in and join them. He took a run

up, jumped and crashed into the sea, which he discovered was extremely shallow at this point. The rest of the team had been crouching down to make it look as though the water was much deeper than it actually was!

During the 1970s, Allan Lamb was playing in a game for Western Province against what was then Rhodesia in the Currie Cup in South Africa. The Western Province captain was Eddie 'Bunter' Barlow. Unfortunately, Barlow and Lamb did not get on and one night during a social gathering, Lamb played a joke on Barlow by pouring flour all over his head.

The generously dusted Barlow was said not to have taken the incident well. And so, the next day, Barlow made Lamb field from fine leg to fine leg for about fifteen overs. The ice was broken when Lamb eventually spotted a bike propped up at the edge of the ground. At the end of one over, Lamb purloined the bike and used it to ride across the pitch to his fielding position.

Once, while away from home, Dickie Bird was staying in a hotel in Northampton. One morning after breakfast and before a hard day's umpiring, Dickie sat reading the newspaper while enjoying a cup of coffee. The tranquil scene was, however, transformed when his newspaper suddenly burst into flames.

Now in a panic, Dickie had to improvise and threw his cup of coffee over the paper to extinguish the flames. Only then did he notice Allan Lamb hiding under his breakfast table with a cigarette lighter in his hand.

Another hotel-based incident was perpetrated on Sky Sports commentator David 'Bumble' Lloyd by Andrew Flintoff and Steve Harmison during a tour of Pakistan in 2005.

Lloyd had put on a pub quiz for the England supporters and travelling media, and one of the prizes on offer was an alarm clock from a mosque, which was designed to wake the user up with the sound of the Muslim call to prayer.

Flintoff and Harmison did not win the quiz and so did not win the prize of the call to prayer alarm clock. Instead, they immediately borrowed the device from its lucky recipient before proceeding to pop to the hotel reception where they obtained Lloyd's room key on false pretences.

The pair snuck into the room without Lloyd's knowledge and heaved the enormous, heavy wardrobe in its corner to one side. They set the call to prayer alarm for four in the morning and positioned it carefully behind the wardrobe. Finally, they heaved the wardrobe back into place and made a sharp exit.

Sure enough, at four o'clock, Lloyd was roused from his slumber by the sound of the call to prayer booming out from behind his wardrobe. Unfortunately for Lloyd, the wardrobe turned out to be too large and heavy for one man to shift on his own.

Luckily, the sound of the call to prayer did not go on too long so he was able to return to his bed and settle back down for what remained of the night.

Or at least he would have done if Flintoff and Harmison hadn't discovered that the clock could be set not just for one but for multiple alarms during the night.

And so Lloyd was called to prayer again at five, then at five-thirty and then again at six o'clock.

All this praying did not seem to do him much good, and Lloyd emerged the next day absolutely shattered from lack of sleep, much to Flintoff and Harmison's amusement.

While in India for the World Cup, Dickie Bird suffered a nasty stomach upset and had to stay in bed in his hotel because he felt so ill. He received a call from Allan Lamb telling him that he had something that he thought would help cure him.

Dickie therefore invited Lamb round to his room. A few minutes later, Lamb appeared, followed by a squad of armed soldiers whom he had found outside the hotel guarding the premises in case of political unrest.

Once the soldiers were lined up around Dickie's bed, Lamby told them: 'Okay, let's put the poor bugger out of his misery! Ready! Aim! Fire!'

Kent and England batsman Rob Key described how Graeme Swann was not just a great cricketer but also a brilliant mimic.

'I remember rooming with Swanny,' Key recalled, 'and every night he would just have conversations with himself, but he was a mimic so he would constantly go from being a male to a female; he would argue with himself in two different characters.'

Swann then put his vocal abilities to work to impersonate David 'Bumble' Lloyd, England's head coach at the time, in a phone call to Kent's David Fulton. Following the best season of his career in 1997, Fulton heard Lloyd's voice telling him that he was going to be selected for England.

Fulton was convinced that he was genuinely talking to Lloyd and was delighted by the news of his call-up. Key said that the impression was so good they had to ring Fulton up again an hour later and tell him he hadn't been called up for England after all and the phone call had just been a prank. It was at that point, Key said, that he started thinking they might have gone a little bit far.

Sadly, Fulton never was called up for England. Or perhaps he did get the call but told the voice on the other end of the phone, 'f*** off! I know it's you again, Swanny!'

England cricketer Tim Bresnan recalls staying in a Durham hotel while playing Australia in a one-day series.

On returning to his room, he discovered a mysterious key card left on his dresser. Bresnan tried it on his own door and then on the door to the next room. The key turned out to work for all the rooms in the hotel. It was a master key presumably accidentally left behind by a cleaner. Bresnan and Jimmy Anderson decided to use the key card to get into their teammate Graeme Swann's room.

'So we waited for Swanny to leave for dinner,' recalled Bresnan, 'and we go into his room and turn the mattress upside down. We put porn on the TV, turned it up full blast. Took the batteries out of the remote. We stole all of his mini-bar ... We ordered some room service ... We basically ransacked his room. Chucked his wardrobe all over the bed and stuff like that. And then we went for dinner.'

Swann then returned to his room with his wife who, unbeknown to Bresnan and Anderson, was also staying with him.

The next day, Swann told the pair of the chaotic scene he and Mrs Swann had found in their room.

'I couldn't get the porn off the TV, lads. I literally couldn't get the porn off the TV.'

The Swanns had to call room service to come and make the bed up for them but still couldn't find any way of switching the porn off on the television.

'All three of us were stood there watching porn while she was making the bed up,' lamented Swann.

So if you ever get caught watching any dodgy TV channels in your hotel room, you could always try blaming it on other mischievous guests in possession of a master key!

STICK IT UP YOUR UMPIRE

'The umpire,' wrote famed cricket correspondent Neville Cardus, 'is like the geyser in the bathroom; we cannot do without it, yet we notice it only when it is out of order.' On the other hand, many people seem to manage without having a geyser in their bathroom or indeed any means to blast thousands of gallons of boiling water into the air without warning. Umpires are, however, essential for avoiding mayhem in the game of cricket. Unless, of course, it's mayhem that they themselves cause. Most importantly, they are there to put even the highest and mightiest of players in their place.

There are many stories of W. G. Grace's reluctance to leave the crease when dismissed. On one occasion, the ball flicked his off stump only for Grace to pick the bail up and put it back in place while remarking nonchalantly, 'Windy day, umpire.'

'Yes,' the umpire agreed. 'Careful it doesn't blow your cap off on the way back to the pavilion.'

Towards the end of his cricketing career, Ian Botham was also beginning to appear on stage in pantomime. His theatrical appearances were sadly not always appreciated by the critics, with one reviewer declaring of his role in *Babes in the Wood*: 'Botham was more wooden than any tree in the forest.'

The world of panto even seemed to follow him on to the cricket pitch. So when Botham rapped a batsman on the pads and shouted "Owzat!', umpire Dickie Bird answered him with a panto-style cry of: 'Oh no, he isn't!'

David 'Bumble' Lloyd recalled a story about Arthur Jepson. Jeppo not only had a twenty-six-year career as an umpire, but he was also a former player for Nottinghamshire CCC as well as Newark Town, Mansfield Town, Grantham Town, Port Vale and Stoke City football clubs.

One time during his umpiring days, Jepson witnessed England bowler Neal Radford struggling to find his rhythm, repeatedly performing, in Lloyd's words, 'a shuffling run to the crease'. After a few minutes of this, Jeppo's booming voice sounded out from his position at square leg with a rather blunt assessment of Radford's efforts.

'Can he bat? 'Cause he can't f***ing bowl. And he runs up like he's shit himself!'

According to one tale, Fred Trueman was once bowling his first delivery of the over to a new batsman. After a loud click, the ball was found nestling in second slip's hands.

"Owzat?' cried Trueman.

'Not out!' said the umpire.

Trueman, now slightly irritated, bowled again.

This time the batsman went on to his back foot with both legs together. He played a defensive stroke but missed and the ball struck him on the pads right in front of the stumps.

"Owzat?' cried Trueman.

'Not out!' said the umpire.

Trueman, now more than a little irritated, sent his third delivery down. This time the ball tore straight through, leaving the wicket spread-eagled and the middle stump uprooted and cartwheeling across the square.

Trueman turned to the umpire and remarked, "We nearly had him that time, didn't we?'

Dickie Bird often told the story of how Allan Lamb had once brought a mobile phone on to the field with him when he walked out to bat back in the days when such devices were the size of bricks.

'He asked me if I could keep it,' said Dickie. 'I wouldn't have it because it was in the middle of a Test.'

Lamb nevertheless insisted on handing over the massive phone for the umpire's safe keeping and, sure enough, after a few minutes, it started ringing, which caused Dickie to jump 'a foot in the air'.

Lamb, at the other end of the pitch, shouted over to him: 'Answer it, Dickie! And tell them I'll ring them back!'

Dickie fumbled around with the phone and eventually managed to answer the call. He then heard Ian Botham's voice from the pavilion.

'Tell that Lamby to play his shots or get out!' said Botham.

At least, that was what was claimed in one version of the story. In another version, Botham asked Dickie what the score was and if he could speak to Lamby.

'Hang on,' Dickie told him. 'He won't be in for long!'

Dickie Bird described the most embarrassing experience of his umpiring career.

At Old Trafford, he had found himself desperate for the toilet. Unfortunately he was part way through umpiring a Test match between England and the West Indies. Ian Botham was bowling and Bird informed him that he had to go off. Botham reminded him that they were in the middle of a Test match only to realize the extent of Dickie's predicament. Botham therefore concluded on a philosophical note saying, 'Well, if you gotta go, you gotta go.'

Bird stopped the match and announced, 'I'm very sorry, gentlemen, but nature calls!' He then scurried away off the pitch only to return a few minutes later through the members' enclosure, zipping up his own personal member's enclosure as he did so. The players were all greatly amused and an enormous roar went up from the crowd.

John Arlott said of umpires that it was rather suitable for them 'to dress like dentists, since one of their tasks is to draw stumps'.

After a career as a colourful Australian cricketer, Cec Pepper switched to being a colourful umpire instead.

In June 1964, in his first season as an umpire, Pepper officiated in a match between Glamorgan and Warwickshire at Ebbw Vale. Glamorgan's batting was a slow and frustrating spectacle for Pepper, who in his playing days had preferred a rather more ostentatious and exciting style. When in their second innings Glamorgan's batsman Bernard Hedges seemed to be blocking everything that came his way, Pepper eventually lost his patience and, while passing bowler Jack Bannister his sweater, told him: 'Hit him on the pad, for God's sake, and I'll give the bugger out.'

Bannister was soon replaced by Tom Cartwright, to whom he apparently passed on Pepper's advice. Cartwright accordingly sent the ball down Hedges' leg side by a good angle and then immediately appealed.

'Not out,' said Pepper with a look of contempt. 'And don't believe everything you hear from that bloody fool Bannister.'

Dickie Bird recounted a story about Cedric Rhodes, who had been chairman of Lancashire CCC. Concerned by ongoing hostility between India and Pakistan, Rhodes asked the team's wicketkeeper Farokh Engineer if he would have to return home to fight for his country.

Engineer replied that if the fighting reached his village, he would then have to go 'to protect my wife and children'.

'Which village is that?' asked Rhodes.

'Altrincham,' responded Engineer.

New Zealand umpire Billy Bowden became known for holding up 'the crooked finger of doom'. Rather than presenting a vertically straight finger when giving a batsman out, his finger went up in the shape of a candy cane. Even when signalling a six, he would hold up both hands and show the crooked finger on each of them.

In fact, the bent fingers turned out not to be an affectation. After ten years as an umpire, Bowden revealed that he had received a diagnosis of rheumatoid arthritis when he was just twenty-two. This condition had put an early end to his career as a fast bowler, and it prevented him from lifting his finger straight over his head, as straightening his fingers was extremely painful.

Former English cricketer and commentator Paul Allott once described to viewers how Zimbabwean umpire Jeff Fenwick gave a player out: 'Umpire Fenwick just twitches his nose, instead of putting his finger up in the usual way.'

Among the many items that Dickie Bird kept in his pockets were a collection of marbles that he used to help count the number of deliveries that had been bowled. In 1995 at Old Trafford, these counters spilled out of his pocket, forcing him to go down on all fours as he attempted to find them again, all the while telling anyone within earshot, 'I've lost my marbles.' No one seemed to be particularly surprised by this revelation.

Phil Tufnell once asked an umpire, 'Are you blind?'

The umpire was unable to believe what he had just heard and responded, 'I beg your pardon?'

'Are you f***ing deaf as well?!' asked Tufnell.

UNFORTUNATE CRICKETING ACCIDENTS

(If Not Tragedies)

The game of cricket is not just an entertaining form of sport; nor is it merely an opportunity for outpourings of insults and abuse; it also provides a means for people to inflict serious injury both on others and occasionally themselves.

The sport's dangers have been apparent since its earliest days. The first organized cricket match recorded in history was played on 10 September 1624 at Horsted Keynes, a small village not far from Ashdown Forest in West Sussex. And the reason we know about this particular match is because it crops up in a coroner's court record. It was the first actual match for which an official record exists because it was also the first cricket match that resulted in the death of one of its players.

The match was between two Sussex villages, Horsted Keynes and West Hoathly, and the cricketer who lost his life was Jasper Vinall. It might be assumed that Vinall died as a result of being struck by a fast-moving ball, but this was not the case. He was dispatched both from the game and from this life, when he received a wallop to the head from a heavy wooden implement.

Edward Tye was batting when Vinall was struck. Tye had already hit the ball in the air but then, in an attempt to save himself from being caught out, tried to give it another almighty whack. As the laws of the game had not at this time been codified, Tye was within his rights to strike the ball a second time. But sadly, in the process, he hit not just the ball but also the skull of one of his fellow players.

So was Vinall an unfortunate fielder attempting to catch Vye out? Possibly not.

The evidence in the coroner's report suggests that the two men may have been on the same team. After suffering his injury, Vinall passed away thirteen days later in West Hoathly. And West Hoathly was coincidentally the home village of batsman Edward Tye. So if Tye and Vinall were on the same team, why was Vinall so close to Tye's bat? All we know is that, following the case's referral to the local coroner's court, the cause of death was ascribed to misadventure.

And then, just twenty-three years later, it happened again. In 1647 in Selsey, on the coast of West Sussex, a cricketer called Henry Brand died after being hit on the head by batsman Thomas Latter. Following this second death, it might be assumed that urgent consideration would be given to the matter of permitting double strikes. It was not until the laws of cricket were codified almost 100 years later, however, that hitting the ball twice was deemed illegal.

According to the laws of the game drawn up in 1744: 'If a Ball is nipp'd up, and he strikes it again wilfully, before it came to the Wicket, it's out,' ruling out such accidents in future. Henceforth, any double strikes would automatically put a batsman out and any future fatalities resulting from the same would presumably be classed as manslaughter.

Dying as a result of involvement in a game of cricket is bad luck enough, but in London in 1731 a Mr Legat suffered an even greater misfortune. According to a contemporary report, Legat was 'a cooper in Basinghall Street' as well as being 'a considerable Dealer in Brandy and Rum', and he was killed when he was hit by a cricket ball despite not playing in the game or even being among its spectators.

Legat's sole mistake was that he chose to pass by at the time of the match. It is recorded that he was 'passing over Moorfields in the Whitsun Holidays' and that he walked along Artillery Road in Finsbury, North London, past the Artillery Ground, which was then the main venue for commercial matches in London.

Sure enough, just as Legat walked by, a ball came sailing out of the arena, causing him 'the Misfortune to be struck with the Ball on the Side of his Nose'. According to this report, the impact 'set him a Bleeding more or less till the Day of his Death; when the bleeding stopt outwardly, he bled inwardly and when stopt inwardly, he bled outwardly'.

Poor Mr Legat passed away a month after his injury had occurred, on 6 July 1731. The cause of death was given, as you may already have guessed, as loss of blood.

As well as hastening the demise of various villagers around the West Sussex area, cricket was also blamed for the death of the Prince of Wales in 1751.

Prince Frederick was the eldest son of King George II and Queen Caroline. He was nevertheless not popular with his parents. When his grandfather George I succeeded to the throne of Great Britain in 1714, the family had to relocate from their native Hanover to London. Or, at least, most of them did. The seven-year-old Prince Frederick was left behind.

He was finally summoned to London in 1728 after his father had become king, thereby making him Prince of Wales and heir to the throne but still his parents did not change their attitude. When his mother lay dying in 1737, George II refused to allow his son to see her on her deathbed, while Queen Caroline commented, 'At least I shall have one comfort in having my eyes eternally closed – I shall never see that monster again.'

Despite being German-born like the rest of his family,

Frederick seemed to become more British than the British. The song 'Rule, Britannia!' was performed for the first time at the prince's Buckinghamshire home Cliveden. It was also in the grounds there that Frederick enjoyed playing cricket with his children. He had played in a 'great Match at Cricket' on Bromley Common in August 1735 when he had led a team of Londoners against the Earl of Middlesex's team from Kent before a crowd of several thousand.

Frederick's London team only managed seventy-three in their first innings, to which Kent replied with ninety-seven. The prince's team added just thirty-two runs in their second outing, leaving the Earl of Middlesex's men able to chase the total down without the loss of another wicket. At this point it was reported that his 'Royal Highness immediately left the Field'.

Unfortunately, this did not turn out to be Prince Frederick's worst cricketing experience. According to legend, he received a blow to the chest while playing the game with his children. This caused an abscess to develop, which was made worse by a chill that he had caught playing tennis. This eventually led to his death when the abscess burst on 31 March 1751.

There had, of course, still been no reconciliation with his father, George II, who refused to attend his son's funeral and even forbade the playing of any music at the service.

Presumably he didn't like cricket very much either.

Cricketing injuries great and small have continued into the modern age. And cricketers themselves may not always be the most sympathetic of individuals.

Fred Trueman once bowled a beamer straight into his England teammate Godfrey Evans, playing for Kent, who suffered three broken ribs as a result. When Evans received an apology from the Yorkshireman, it was expressed in Trueman's unique manner: 'Sorry about your ribs, Godders. Really I meant to skull you. Anyway, why didn't you put your bloody bat there?'

Harold Larwood was not only a terrifying bowler to face during the bodyline tour in Australia, he also bowled just as fiercely in domestic matches. On one occasion he bowled and hit Wilfred Rhodes, who was twenty-seven years his senior, on the foot.

Rhodes took off his pad, boot and sock, and rolled on the ground in agony. The umpire came over to Rhodes to assess what had happened and to ask if he thought he could walk.

'Yes,' gasped Rhodes still in enormous pain.

'Good,' said the umpire. 'In that case, walk back to the pavilion. You're out!'

In 1980, David Lloyd had a small chance of being named England captain. He hoped therefore that his performance against the West Indies in a one-day international at Headingley would help his cause. Unfortunately, he then found himself batting against Malcolm Marshall. Marshall walked so far to begin his run up that Lloyd commented afterwards, 'I don't go that far on my holidays.'

Marshall came thundering in, launching the ball at Lloyd who played what he described as 'a very hurried backward defensive prod'. It obviously wasn't defensive enough, as the ball smashed into him and broke his arm in two places.

Lloyd was helped away off the pitch, thinking to himself, 'I wonder if I've done enough?'

Brian Johnston once commented that 'batsmen wear so much protection these days that I mostly identify them from their posteriors.'

During the 1974 Ashes, David Lloyd made a rash claim to his fellow players. He told them that he could play Aussie fast bowler Jeff Thomson 'with my dick'.

Sure enough, when he went out to bat in the second innings, Lloyd made seventeen before a ball from Thomson shot through and caught him right in the abdominal protector.

In Richie Benaud's telling of the tale, Lloyd was then 'airlifted' back to the dressing room, where his first words were: 'See! Told you I could!'

Lloyd presumably gasped these triumphal words with a look of some discomfort. The delivery from Thomson had not just dented his cricket box, it had also turned it inside out. 'Every bit of me that had begun on the inside,' he said, 'was now on the outside.' He later added: 'I didn't need a doctor; I needed a welder.'

Cricketer Rachael Heyhoe Flint was being interviewed when she was asked if batters in the women's game still wore boxes.

'Oh yes,' she replied, 'but we call them manhole covers.'

England cricketer Brian Close was fielding near to the wicket at short leg. The batsman struck the ball and it flew straight into the side of Close's face. Incredibly, the ball then hurtled up into the air and the batsman was caught at slip.

One of the other fielders was concerned about the ball hitting Close in the head. 'What would have happened if he'd hit you right between the eyes?' asked the fielder.

'In that case,' said Close, 'he'd have been caught at cover.'

W. G. Grace played cricket as an amateur while his profession was that of a medical doctor. A fielder caught him out but struck his head on a jutting piece of metal in the process. Luckily, Doctor Grace was able to provide first aid as he passed by on his way back to the pavilion.

During a match at Old Trafford in 1887, A. C. M. Croome, a former Gloucestershire player, somehow cut his throat on a jagged metal railing. Once again, the good doctor was on hand after his afternoon's bowling and probably saved Croome's life when he spent a full half-hour holding the man's gashed throat together until the bleeding stopped.

Broadcaster Jo Sheldon once reported: 'A brain scan revealed that Andrew Caddick is not suffering from a fracture of the shin.'

Following an injury, Andrew Flintoff commented: 'In the past five weeks I've trained hard, trying to get my ankle back to where I want it to be.'

The West Indies batsman Lawrence Rowe was considered by Michael Holding to be one of the greatest he had ever seen. He scored a double hundred and another hundred in his Test debut against New Zealand and famously used to whistle after every shot like a jolly carefree workman going about his day. Despite his brilliance on the pitch, Rowe suffered from at least two conditions that were supremely unfortunate for a cricketer: he had problems with his eyesight and he was allergic to grass.

Rowe recalled, 'I was sneezing and my eyes were itching, sometimes I'd go into bat and couldn't see anything.'

Although this ironic allergy might seem comical, it of course denied Rowe his chance to become one of cricket's all-time greats, and he finished with 2047 Test runs at an average of 43.55.

Bruce French was England's wicketkeeper during the 1987–88 tour of Pakistan. One day during the tour, French was standing minding his own business watching a net session. When the ball flew out among the spectators, one helpful soul decided to return it, but in the process of throwing it back, accidentally whopped French on the head.

French had to be taken to hospital for treatment, where he managed to get injured yet again when he was hit by a car while he was standing outside the main entrance.

French finally got inside the hospital to have stitches to

UNFORTUNATE CRICKETING ACCIDENTS

repair the damage the ball had done to his brow. He was checked over and thankfully the injury was not found to be serious. After his examination was concluded, French stood up and immediately pranged his head yet again on a low-hanging light fitting.

Chris Old was a fine quick bowler who made his debut for Yorkshire in 1966, where he was seen by many as being Fred Trueman's natural successor. He went on to play forty-six Tests and thirty-two one-day internationals for England, but he also became renowned for his habit of acquiring injuries at unfortunate moments. He had operations on both knees in 1970 and 1971, and faced the possibility of major surgery in 1976, which threatened to leave him confined to a wheelchair.

Famously, the first bowling machine to be installed at Lord's was given the name Chris Old in his honour. Why? Because it kept breaking down all the time.

The ailments of the England side were once so extensive that Martin Johnson summed them up in the *Independent* by saying: '[Mark] Ilott is out of this game with a groin strain and thus joins Darren Gough, Chris Lewis and Andrew Caddick on the list of those more in line for a trip to Lourdes rather than Lord's.'

England's Andy Lloyd played in one Test match – against the West Indies at Edgbaston in 1984. He batted for thirty-three minutes and made ten runs before misjudging a ball from fast bowler Malcolm Marshall and being hit on the head. Or, to be more precise, on the helmet. He nevertheless spent the next few days in hospital and did not play again in 1984.

His unfortunate injury did, however, leave Lloyd as the holder of one impressive record. He is the only batsman in history to open in a Test innings and never be dismissed.

In 1906, the then thirty-five-year-old George Hirst became the first and only cricketer to take 200 wickets and score 2,000 runs in one season. Hirst was asked how he thought another cricketer would feel if they ever managed to match his record.

'Bloody tired,' he said.

George Hirst was so prolific a batsman and bowler that he developed a significant knee problem and had to massage his sore feet each morning and night with neatsfoot oil (oil made from the shin bones and feet of cattle, which is usually used to help preserve leather). When Hirst complained to his doctor about the state of his feet, the medic replied: 'Don't you realize, Mr Hirst: you've given your legs more use than five ordinary men in a lifetime.'

While the great cricketer W. G. Grace is remembered as a legendary and pivotal figure in the history of the game, there were two other Grace brothers who also played at the highest level, but the career of one of them was cut tragically short.

England played Australia at the Oval on 6–8 September 1880. The match was retrospectively recognized as being the first Test match to be played on English soil. The event was also unique because the England team featured all three Grace brothers. The eldest of the three was E. M. Grace, then there was W. G., and the youngest was Fred. England went on to win the match. During its course, W. G. made 152 and so became the first Englishman to have scored a hundred on his Test debut. Fred, for his part, was less fortunate in the batting stakes. He chalked up a duck in each innings in this, his one appearance in a Test match. He did, however, take a clean catch off George Bonnor while Australia's batsmen were attempting a third run. Six years later, Barclay's *Book of Cricket* described this as being 'the most famous deep-field catch in history'.

Unfortunately, Fred did not live to hear this appreciation of his skills. He had gone on to play the very next day for Gloucestershire against a local team in Stroud. He then moved on to Basingstoke, where he was due to play a benefit match on 15 September, although by this stage he had become unwell and had to be persuaded not to play. On 17 September, Fred was diagnosed with pneumonia. He had caught a cold during the Test match and then been soaked by rainy weather during the match at Stroud. He died on the 22 September aged just twenty-nine. He was the first – and so far only – cricketer to have died two weeks after his last international match.

On a slightly cheerier note, cricketing injuries have also been the subject of many great cricketing jokes.

> **A priest goes to visit a man who is grieving over the death of his aged father.**
>
> **'I'm so sorry to hear of your loss,' says the priest. 'Did you try taking your father to Lourdes like I suggested?'**
>
> **'Yes, I did,' replies the man. 'But we'd only been there a few minutes when he passed away.'**
>
> **'Was it his heart?' asks the priest.**
>
> **'No, father,' replies the man. 'He got hit on the head by a cricket ball.'**

A batsman gets hit on the head by a bouncer and has to retire as he is suffering from concussion. Later in the match, a wicket falls and the coach asks the team physio if the batsman is fit enough to return to the crease.

'He's still a bit dazed,' says the physio. 'He's not sure who he is.'

'That's excellent,' says the coach. 'Tell him he's Ricky Ponting and then get him back out there.'

A man goes to the doctor and says, 'Doctor, doctor, I've got a cricket ball stuck up my backside.'

'How's that?' asks the doctor.

'Don't you start!' says the man.

IT'S JUST NOT CRICKET …
OR IS IT?

C ricket is synonymous with the concept of gentlemanly fair play even to those who know nothing about the game. Those who do know something about it, meanwhile, know that one or two cricketers enjoy bending the rules ever so slightly when the opportunity arises.

And it seems that some of them have been trying to get away with this for many hundreds of years.

The maximum permitted width of a cricket bat is 108 mm (4¼ inches). This law was first laid down in 1774 in the wake of what became known as the 'monster bat controversy'.

On 23 September 1771, during a match against Hambledon, a Thomas 'Daddy' White was playing for Chertsey. When White took the crease, he came armed with a bat so enormous it was as wide as the wicket. The bat was believed to have been about 2 feet across.

If this was meant to be a joke, the Hambledon players were not amused. They protested and Mr White had his bat shaved down to half its size there and then before his eyes. Hambledon later had an iron frame made to check the dimensions of bats in future.

Well, it was either that or make the wicket much wider.

During the 1990–91 Ashes, England opening batsman Michael Atherton stood his ground after apparently getting an edge and the ball being caught behind by wicketkeeper Ian Healy. A loud appeal followed but Atherton was given not out.

Healy promptly told Atherton, 'You're a f***ing cheat!'

'Well,' Atherton responded, 'when in Rome, dear boy!'

According to Henry Blofeld, Atherton's words left Healy feeling a little confused. 'Mate, I don't get it,' he said. 'We're playing in Sydney.'

In 1947, England were playing Australia at Adelaide and were already down 2–0 in that year's Ashes. On the third day, England's lead was over 300, Denis Compton was nearing a century and the Australians were becoming frustrated. The thirty-eight-year-old Donald Bradman was fielding at cover point when he saw the ball hit Compton's pad.

'Howzat!' called Bradman.

Compton asked, 'Don, how could you possibly see from out there?'

'I couldn't,' Bradman answered, 'but it might have been out, mightn't it? That's for umpires to decide, not me!'

Dickie Bird described in his book of anecdotes *White Cap and Bails* an incident that occurred while the future umpire David Shepherd was playing for Gloucestershire against Derbyshire. Shepherd gloved a ball from Keith Stevenson, thereby enabling Bob Taylor to take the catch.

'You gloved that, you bugger!' cried Bird.

'I know I gloved it, Dickie,' said Shepherd. 'You know I gloved it. But nobody else does. There was no appeal. So I'm not going to walk, am I?'

Bird then informed Bob Taylor that Shepherd had just 'gloved that'.

'Get away,' said Taylor, 'you're having me on.'

'You ask him, then,' said Bird.

Taylor proceeded to do just that and received an honest reply from Shepherd: "Course I gloved it! But nobody appealed. So I'm staying put!'

Early in his career, future bodyline bowler Harold Larwood was playing for Nottinghamshire against Yorkshire at Bramall Lane, Sheffield. It was a bright day and as Larwood ran up to bowl against Herbert Sutcliffe, at the time one of England's most accomplished and consistent run-makers, something happened that made the batsman draw away. Sutcliffe had been distracted by the sight of an object flashing in the crowd. Larwood discovered that this had been the sun reflecting on the metal clasp on a handbag belonging to his mother, who was sitting in the crowd.

He said that at first he didn't dare admit it had been his mother who had caused the stoppage but when Sutcliffe eventually found out the truth, he told Larwood: 'Youngster, don't expect your mother to help get you wickets!'

There is one man in particular who exemplified the habit of bending the rules of cricket to his own advantage. And he's possibly the most famous player in the history of the game.

W. G. Grace dominated cricket during his lifetime in the late nineteenth and early twentieth centuries, and is regarded by some as an almost god-like figure in the history of the sport. Indeed, Terry Gilliam adapted a photo of W. G. Grace to create the animated face of God who speaks from the clouds to King Arthur in the 1975 film *Monty Python and the Holy Grail.*

It is therefore surprising to remember that Grace was not a professional cricketer and that he played exclusively as an amateur throughout his life. The MCC had picked up on his potential and crowd-pulling popularity when he was a teenager and thus made him a member at a very young age. Grace therefore said that he would play as an amateur according to the MCC's dictum that 'a gentleman ought not to make any profit from playing cricket'. As things turned out, however, Grace made a very handsome profit from the sport.

Initially he found that he couldn't afford to play as an amateur and an unspoken agreement was therefore established that Grace would break the essential rule of being an amateur. He would start taking money. And, as things turned out, he took quite a lot of it.

Grace would often refuse to tour unless some form of compensation could be offered. Grace thus went on to make a vast fortune via expenses claims for travel and accommodation. Grace's expenses turned out to far exceed the income of professional players of the time.

On one occasion, for example, Grace managed to extract a fee of £1,500 for a tour (the equivalent of over £150,000 today). He took a thirteen-strong team with him on tour in 1891–92 but pocketed 20 per cent of the cost of supporting them for himself.

One of Grace's most famous lines supposedly occurred after he strode out to bat in a match only to be bowled out on the first ball.

Grace simply picked up the bails and replaced them on the stumps while pronouncing: 'They came to see me bat, not you bowl!' An alternative version of the quote is given as: 'They came to see me bat, not you umpire!'

At the same time as claiming extraordinary levels of expenses for his cricketing appearances, W. G. Grace was also extremely generous. Some might say he could afford to be thanks to all the money he was making. Nevertheless, he would also help those in need and did not insist on charging his medical patients if they were short of funds.

Once Grace even treated a man who had attempted to burgle his house. The desperate individual had attempted to raid Grace's larder only to have a heavy sash window fall right on his hands. Grace's brother E. M. returned home a little later in the day and asked what had happened, and if the intruder had been handed over to the police.

W. G. replied, 'Medical etiquette! I dressed his wounds. First-class job, too. But hand him over? Oh no! Not my patient! I just went round and gave him a running kick and let him go.'

The toss was the first code in the earliest laws of cricket laid down in 1744: 'The Pitching the first Wicket is to be determined by the Toss of a Piece of Money.'

The tradition has continued ever since, standing the test of time. It was nonetheless the subject of some abuse by W. G. The British coin used for the toss in Grace's day had the queen's head on one side and an image of Britannia on the other. Grace, therefore, did not call heads or tails in response to the toss but rather for 'the Lady', which was correct in all circumstances. He would then pick up the coin, announce his team would be batting and march swiftly away before anyone dared challenge him.

In case there was ever any doubt about who should bat first, Grace also pronounced: 'When you win the toss – bat. If you are in doubt, think about it, then bat. If you have very big doubts, consult a colleague, then bat.'

And: 'When I win the toss on a good pitch, I bat. When I win the toss on a doubtful pitch, I think about it a bit and then I bat. When I win the toss on a very bad pitch, I think about it a bit longer and then I bat.'

W. G. Grace went in to bat in a county match. He whacked the ball right up into the air and managed to make one run, only to notice that the ball was heading straight towards a fielder's outstretched hands. And so, instead of going for a second, the good doctor swiftly declared before the ball dropped from the sky. When it finally fell into the fielder's waiting palms, a cry of howzat went up, but Grace was able to argue successfully that the catch didn't count because it had happened following close of play.

Another of W. G. Grace's little tricks was to distract the opposing team by pointing out an imaginary flock of geese flying across the sky almost exactly where the sun was.

'Did you see them?' he would ask. 'Pity! They've just gone behind the trees!' Grace would then whisper to the bowler, 'Quick, Fred! Slip him a fast one on leg stump!' while the batsman was still dazzled from staring directly into the sun in the hope of catching sight of a few geese.

In another famous tale, W. G. Grace intimidated an umpire into turning down appeal after appeal made against him for LBW during the course of a match. Finally, he was clearly bowled out by Charles Kortright, who knocked down two of his stumps.

Grace began his walk back to the pavilion only to hear Kortright call after him: 'Surely you're not going, doctor! There's one stump still standing!'

One of W. G. Grace's most infamous and outrageous acts was his 'kidnapping' of the Australian player Billy Midwinter in June 1878.

According to the story, Midwinter was due to play for Australia against Middlesex at Lord's when he was bundled into a cab by W. G. and taken to the Oval to play for Gloucestershire against Surrey instead. Midwinter's Australian teammates followed in pursuit in their own cab and had a frank exchange of views with Grace at the Oval.

In the short description of this tale, however, not only should the word 'kidnapping' be shown in quotation marks but also, perhaps, should the word 'Australian'. Billy Midwinter was born in 1851 in St Briavels in the Forest of Dean, Gloucestershire. His birthplace was therefore only about twenty-three miles from that of Grace in Downend. When he was nine, Midwinter emigrated to Australia where he played for Victoria before joining the national side for two Tests in 1876–77. After this, he joined Gloucestershire where he took twenty-nine wickets in nine matches and made 183 runs. When Gloucestershire turned up at the Oval they were therefore a man short.

Grace ultimately won the battle for Midwinter and dubbed the troublesome Australians 'a damned lot of sneaks'. Gloucestershire nevertheless went on to lose their match, with Midwinter making only four runs in his first innings and a duck in his second. Australia, meanwhile, won their match by ninety-eight runs.

Australia's manager wrote a strongly worded letter of complaint about Grace's behaviour. Further letters were exchanged until Grace wrote with a plea to let 'bygones be bygones' while offering his regret and apologies for his 'unparliamentary language' during the exchanges outside the Oval.

Midwinter didn't play again for Australia that season and instead continued to play for his county side before being picked for England, for whom he played four Test matches against Australia in 1881–82. After this, he emigrated back to Australia where he rejoined Victoria and played in a series of Test matches for the Australian national side once again.

Midwinter is therefore the only cricketer to play for both Australia and England in Test matches against each other. Unfortunately, his story does not have a happy end, as just a few years after his return to Australia, Midwinter became 'hopelessly insane' and died at the Kew Lunatic Asylum in Melbourne in December 1890.

Even the historic Ashes rivalry between Australia and England has its roots in a piece of gamesmanship by W. G. Grace.

On 28 and 29 August 1882, England played Australia at the Oval. An extraordinary twenty wickets fell on the first day. Australia had gone in to bat first but collapsed for just sixty-three. England then proceeded to not do much better and ended all out for 101. This was despite the presence of W. G., who was bowled by the Australian captain Fred Spofforth for just four runs.

During the course of the day, the English captain A. N. 'Monkey' Hornby had stepped out of his crease to do a bit of gardening – that is, using his bat to prod and push the pitch, which was damp from a recent burst of rain. Spofforth decided not to run Hornby out during this period of horticultural endeavour. This sportsmanlike gesture was sadly not to be reciprocated.

On the second day, despite rain delaying play, Australia improved their form, but their tailender Sammy Jones repeated what Hornby had done the day before. Assuming the ball to be dead, Jones exchanged a look with Grace, who gave him a nod of understanding. Jones then felt safe to step out from the crease. He proceeded to do his own bit of gardening, at which point Grace immediately used the ball in his hand to knock the bails off. Jones was out.

Spofforth made a furious visit to the England dressing room to call Grace a cheat. He then unleashed an equally furious spell of bowling. England needed just eighty-five to win the match. They got to 51 for 2 with Grace not out for thirty-two. The bowling of Australia's Harry Boyle then swiftly saw both George Ulyett and Grace out. England still needed only thirty-two runs to win and had six wickets in hand. Unfortunately, the England runs had dried up.

After sixteen maiden overs interrupted by just one solitary run, England found themselves 66 for 5. Soon after they were 70 for 7, then 75 for 8. They still needed just ten runs. They didn't manage it. They were finally all out for 77, the last eight wickets having all gone for just twenty-six runs.

The tension among the spectators was so great that one man died of a burst blood vessel during the match while another was said to have chewed through the handle of his umbrella (which he presumably had needed because of all the rain both before and during the Test).

On 2 September, a few days after England's shock defeat, the *Sporting Times* printed a mock obituary:

In Affectionate Remembrance

OF

ENGLISH CRICKET,

WHICH DIED AT THE OVAL

ON

29th AUGUST, 1882,

Deeply lamented by a large circle of sorrowing friends and acquaintances.

R.I.P.

N.B.—The body will be cremated and the ashes taken to Australia.

This humorous piece clearly caught public attention not just in the UK but also further afield. Just a few months later, in December 1882, the England team went to Australia on a tour that was billed as an attempt to reclaim the ashes. The team did not on this occasion include Grace, as the doctor had asked for £3,000 to cover his costs of going and this turned out to be five times more than anyone else in the team was receiving.

At a dinner to welcome the team Down Under, Ivo Bligh, the England captain, declared his men had come to 'beard the kangaroo in his den and try and recover those ashes'. England accordingly won the three-match series 2–1. The notion of the ashes then unexpectedly became reality when the team played a country-house match at Rupertswood in Sunbury, Victoria.

Rupertswood was the home of Sir William Clarke, the then president of that other MCC (the Melbourne Cricket Club), and it was here that Sir William's wife Janet, Lady Clarke, along with Florence Morphy and other local society ladies, presented Bligh with a special prize that they had created for him. This was a tiny terracotta urn about 10.5 cm high supposedly containing the hitherto fictional ashes.

The presentation is said by some to have occurred on Christmas Eve 1882, although it may have been given when the England team next visited Sir William at Easter 1883. Indeed, an indication of the urn's date of origin is suggested by the two labels pasted on its side. One of these simply reads 'The Ashes', while the other is a verse cut out from the Melbourne edition of *Punch* magazine, which had been published on 1 February 1883:

'When Ivo goes back with the urn, the urn;
Studds, Steel, Read and Tylecote return, return;
The welkin will ring loud,
The great crowd will feel proud,
Seeing Barlow and Bates with the urn, the urn;
And the rest coming home with the urn.'

The Ashes were taken back to England in triumph. Bligh returned to Australia the following year and this time brought back Ashes-bearer Florence Morphy with him, the couple having married on 9 February 1884.

The exact nature of the ashes contained in the urn remains a subject of debate. At first they were believed to be the remains of the ball from the country-house match in which the team had just played. The story was then changed and they were claimed to be the ashes of one of the bails that had been burnt following the match. Still later they were said to be the remains of a veil worn by Florence Morphy. Then, just to confuse things even more, Bligh's parlour maid knocked over the urn one day and spilled the contents everywhere. Bligh's butler was then summoned to sort the problem out, which he is said to have done by scooping up some ashes from the fireplace.

After Bligh's death in 1927, the Ashes were left to the MCC. The urn has thus remained permanently at Lord's ever since, apart from a couple of occasions when Australia won the ashes and the MCC allowed the urn to go on a brief, well-guarded trip Down Under before being safely returned.

So for more than 130 years Australia and England have battled for the world's smallest professional sports trophy, which very possibly contains some random detritus from a fireplace and which all has its roots in an appalling piece of behaviour by W. G. Grace!

ALL FACULTIES WORKING PERFECTLY

Everyone engaged in a professional game of cricket naturally always has possession of exceptional physical, sensory and mental abilities. Or do they ... ?

Brian Johnston told a story of an occasion when Middlesex were playing Surrey at Lord's. Pat Pocock strode out to bat for the first time wearing a pair of glasses. Middlesex's bowler Fred Titmus was surprised at the sight and asked, 'What have you got those things on the end of your nose for?'

'Because I'm bloody deaf. Why do you think?' replied Pocock in a somewhat tetchy manner.

He was then bowled out on the first delivery. 'You didn't hear that one too well, did you?' remarked Titmus.

In his book *White Cap and Bails*, Dickie Bird relates a tale about Essex's captain and wicketkeeper Brian 'Tonker' Taylor.

Taylor once tried to trick a batsman into getting himself out. During one over, he moved square leg a little deeper after each ball. The fourth ball was a bouncer, which the batsman hooked high only to be caught just inside the ropes. The umpire, however, called a no ball.

He was tackled over this decision but declared, in his defence, that it was Taylor's fault because he currently had three men behind square leg, while the laws only allowed for two. When asked to point out the third of these men, the umpire indicated a figure standing on the boundary edge.

'Don't tell me you were counting that chap!' cried Taylor. 'That's not a fielder, you fool – that's the bloody ice-cream man!'

In June 1930, Nottinghamshire played Somerset at Taunton. Cecil Charles Coles Case, known as Box Case, walked out to bat against Nottinghamshire's fast bowler Bill Voce. When Voce's ball came at him faster than he had expected, Case tried to get out of the way and in the process manage to collapse on to the stumps.

He then picked himself up and began making his way back to the pavilion when he heard the Nottinghamshire captain Arthur Carr call after him: 'Would you mind leaving us that stump and taking your bat instead?'

In his embarrassment, Case had indeed picked up one of the stumps rather than his bat and was in the process of carrying it away with him as he walked sadly off the pitch.

Keith Miller served as captain for New South Wales but was often rather vague with the directions he gave his men. He would, for example, tell them simply to 'scatter' themselves around the field. Once, having forgotten to name his team's twelfth man, he found twelve players on the field. Miller eventually came up with a cunning solution to the problem.

'It seems we have too many men out here,' he said. 'So will one of you blokes p**s off?'

Several alternative versions of this story exist, with the difference usually being the final two words variously reported as 'bugger off' or 'f*** off'. Or perhaps each of these variations really did occur but on different occasions!

In another story related by Dickie Bird, Keith Miller once had the opposite problem. He arrived for a match and was asked where one of his men was.

'No idea,' said Miller. 'Is he supposed to be playing today?'

'Yes,' came the reply. 'And you were supposed to be giving him a lift!'

In July 1872, Bob Carpenter – then aged forty-one – got the chance to play alongside W. G. Grace in a match between England and a combined team of Nottinghamshire and Yorkshire.

Carpenter was pleased at the news, as he had just played against Grace, and remarked that he had had 'about enough of fielding out to Mr Grace this week; but thank goodness I shall be on his side the next match'.

When Carpenter went out to bat with Grace, England were 77 for 2. Together they added 100 in the next hour before Carpenter was dismissed. During the course of their partnership, Carpenter discovered something about Grace's style.

When a teammate told him he should feel happy with the day's play, Carpenter replied: 'Feel happy! If I had been in much longer I should have died. It is a deal harder work to be in with him than fielding against him. When you are fielding you do get a rest now and again, but when batting you never do!'

Indeed, he and Grace may have put on 100 but they had done so without any hits to the boundary.

Sometimes balls may be lost in a cricket match, but in August 1921 Leicestershire lost an entire player.

They were playing at the Oval in the penultimate round of the County Championship and Surrey, the home team, were desperate to win. By the end of their second innings, they had set Leicestershire a target of 335. At the end of the day, the Leicestershire wicketkeeper Tom Sidwell was not out for one when stumps were pulled.

When play resumed the next day, Sidwell failed to arrive at the Oval in time. The unfortunate man had decided to make his own way to the ground that morning but had managed to get lost on the London Underground system. Sidwell was at first considered retired so he would be able to resume his innings as soon as he found his way on to the Northern Line and arrived back at the Oval. However, the Surrey captain Percy Fender insisted that Sidwell be declared out and thus not allowed to bat again. Surrey went on to win the match but they lost that year's County Championship to Middlesex.

England's legendary batsman Denis Compton hosted a magnificent party on 23 May 1967 at the Hilton Hotel in London to celebrate his fiftieth birthday. Halfway through proceedings, Denis was summoned away to take a phone call.

He returned a few minutes later to tell the assembled multitude that an unexpected problem had arisen with regard to the celebrations.

'That was my mother,' announced Compton. 'She says I'm only forty-nine!'

WHEN THINGS GO WELL
ON THE FIELD

A ll sorts of things can happen on the cricket field. And, despite the way events in the sport can often seem, these don't all involve disasters, humiliation, verbal abuse and swearing. So, let's have a quick look at some happier moments from the annals of cricket.

Harold Larwood married his wife Lois in 1927. A year later, their first child was born and Larwood received the news of the birth by telegram while he was playing against Hampshire at Trent Bridge. When he saw Larwood with the telegram, the Nottinghamshire captain Arthur Carr told him that he should be 'concentrating on the match, not reading messages'.

Larwood replied that he had a baby daughter and punched the air in his excitement. He then proceeded to remove Alexander Hosie, Lewis Harfield, and Percy

Lawrie in just four balls. Their fellow Hampshire batsman Phil Mead survived to make 89 not out and commented as he returned to the pavilion: 'Thank God it wasn't twins!'

The Jamaican cricketer Chris Gayle played for the West Indies from 1998 and captained the Test team from 2007 to 2010. In 2009, he achieved one of the five fastest centuries in Test match history and in 2010 became, after Don Bradman, Brian Lara and Virender Sehwag, the fourth cricketer to have scored two triple centuries in Test cricket. In 2012, during a match against Bangladesh and facing debutant bowler Sohag Gazi, Gayle hit a six off the game's first ball. It was the first time this had happened in the then 137-year history of Test cricket.

In February 2016, the New Zealand captain Brendan McCullum was playing at Hagley Oval in Christchurch in the second Test against Australia. It was McCullum's 101st Test and his last international match. McCullum went in when New Zealand were 32 for 3 after 19.4 overs and proceeded to turn the game on its head.

He hit a century off fifty-four balls and in so doing recorded the fastest century in Test history. The previous record was fifty-six balls and had been jointly held by Viv Richards and Misbah-ul-Haq.

It was an extraordinary achievement but sadly not enough to prevent Australia winning the Test and thereby regaining the top spot in world rankings.

Fred Trueman described an occasion during an Ashes test when England were fielding.

'I went back to my mark and hurtled into the wicket. A rap on the pads. Howzat? One for none. I went back to my mark and hurtled into the wicket and the bails were off – two for none. Then in came the great Sir Don Bradman. I went back to my mark and hurtled into the wicket, the ball was in the air, a fantastic catch on the long-on boundary … three for three hundred and seventy-six.'

In 1934, Australia was playing Worcestershire and Don Bradman was on the second of three consecutive double centuries he made against the county when a voice from the crowd yelled out: 'Give him 300 and ask him to go out!'

Similarly, in January 1930, when Bradman scored 452 not out in 415 minutes for New South Wales against Queensland, one supporter remarked: 'Why don't they let someone else have a turn? I am sick of looking at him.'

In July 1956, England spinner Jim Laker achieved extraordinary figures at Old Trafford, taking 19 wickets in a match for just 90 runs. On his way home, Laker stopped for a drink at a pub in Lichfield. Times then being rather different than today, he was able to sit and enjoy his drink completely undisturbed.

Eventually he arrived home, where he was greeted by his Austrian wife, who knew nothing about cricket and who had therefore been mystified by the many congratulatory phone messages she had been receiving.

'Did you do something good today?' she asked.

Former England captain Alec Stewart achieved a total of 8,463 runs during his Test career from 1990 to 2003. That many runs is remarkable in itself, but it's even more remarkable when you consider that Stewart was born on the 8 April 1963. Or, to put it another way, 8/4/63.

George Hirst was an all-rounder who played for Yorkshire from 1891 to 1921 (with an encore in 1929) and for England from 1897 to 1909. He said (perhaps on more than one occasion): 'Cricket is a game, not a competition. And, when you're both a bowler and a batter, you're twice as happy. You enjoy yourself twice as much.'

WHEN THINGS GO LESS WELL

In life it is important to look on the bright side and to avoid dwelling on the negative. Cricket, however, is considerably more difficult than normal life and thus the moments when things don't go quite as intended have to be faced all too often!

Greg Chappell once commented of his own form: 'I can't really say I'm batting badly. I'm not batting long enough to be batting badly.'

On one occasion, Monty Panesar revealed: 'I have prepared for the worst-case scenario ... But it could be even worse than that.'

When he played for Somerset against Surrey, the future cricket writer R. C. Robertson-Glasgow found it hard going bowling against Jack Hobbs and Andy Sandham. He described it as like 'trying to bowl against God on concrete'.

In 1968, the Welsh bowler Malcolm Nash was hit for six sixes in the course of one over by Gary Sobers. Nash was philosophical in his reflections on the event: 'I suppose I can gain some consolation from the fact that my name will be permanently in the record books.'

During the 1999 World Cup, Steve Waugh made a comment to South Africa's Herschelle Gibbs that has gone down in history.

When Gibbs dropped a catch off Waugh while the Aussie was on his way to a century, Waugh told him: 'Herschelle, you do realize you've just dropped the World Cup, don't you?'

Unfortunately for Gibbs, Australia did indeed go on to win the tournament.

In 1961, Raman Subba Row had failed to hold on to a catch off Fred Trueman's bowling and let the ball go through his legs.

Subba Row told Trueman, 'Sorry, Fred. I should have kept my legs together.'

'Not you, son,' replied Trueman. 'Your mother should have.'

David Sheppard began his Test cricket career in 1950 while still studying at Cambridge University. In 1955 he was ordained as a cleric in the Church of England and ultimately became Bishop of Liverpool. He is to date the only ordained minister to have played in a Test match.

He took a sabbatical from his clerical work to join England for a tour of Australia in 1962–63. Slightly rusty after his time away from the first-class game, he dropped a number of catches. After one of these misses, the bowler Fred Trueman gave him a few words of advice: 'Kid yourself it's Sunday, Rev, and keep your hands together!'

Allan Lamb recalled Dennis Lillee tackling him over his batting. Lamb said he had been playing and repeatedly missing until Lillee called to him and said, 'Hey, mate. Do me a favour. Just hold the bat still and I'll aim at the f***ing thing!'

When Graham Gooch faced Merv Hughes and played and missed several deliveries, Hughes asked him: 'Would you like me to bowl a piano – and see if you can play that?!'

During the second Ashes Test at Lord's in 1989, England batsman Robin Smith played and missed. Aussie fast bowler Merv Hughes then informed Smith, 'You can't f***ing bat.'

On the next ball, Smith hit Hughes for four, which gave the batsman an opportunity for a rejoinder: 'Hey, Merv! We make a fine pair! I can't f***ing bat and you can't f***ing bowl!'

Smith faced Hughes again four years later. Hughes told him, 'It's four years since I bowled to you and you haven't improved.'

Smith then hit Hughes for four before informing him: 'Neither have you.'

Alan McGilvray famously summed up fellow Aussie Kim Hughes' poor batting performance during a match in 1980–81. 'It has been a week of delight and disappointment for Kim Hughes,' announced McGilvray. 'His wife presented him with a pair of twins yesterday ... and a duck today.'

In June 2019 in Kigali City, Rwanda, the Mali women's cricket side appeared in their first ever international match as part of the Kwibuka Twenty20 tournament. They won the toss and opted to bat first against the home side. Mali went on to achieve a landmark record in the history of the sport. Unfortunately, it was not a landmark record that anyone would have wanted.

During the course of nine overs, only one player on the team, Mariam Samake, scored a run, and by the end of the innings lower-order batswoman Balkissa Coulibaly remained not out on 0 runs. In between, their nine teammates were dismissed one by one for a duck each. In the end Mali were bowled out for just six runs.

It was the first time there had been nine ducks on the scorecard in an international cricket match. This was, however, a story of triumph and wholly admirable cricketing spirit. Cricket had been unknown in Mali before 2001. The country had no pitches and no suppliers of cricketing equipment, and the team had very little in the way of financial resources. Only three members of the team were aged over twenty, with Balkissa Coulibaly being just fourteen years old. They went as a learning experience and vowed to play 'even if we have to die'.

The team were awarded the tournament's fair play trophy. They returned home having taken lessons from the tournament, looking to the future of Malian cricket with optimism and hopefully having earned the respect of cricket fans around the world.

In 2006, Goldsborough 2nd XI played Dishforth in the Nidderdale Amateur Cricket League. The result became a famous news story. Goldsborough's innings lasted just twelve short overs and the final scoreboard read 5 runs for 10 wickets. Unfortunately, none of the five runs had been scored with the bat, but instead ten of Goldsborough's batsmen had been out for a duck with the last man left stranded on zero, although the team had managed to clock up five extras.

Their captain Peter Horseman commented on proceedings: 'It was surreal and embarrassing. We almost got a run, but the batsman turned it down because he'd just been hit on the foot.'

Dishforth then proceeded to quickly knock off the six runs required for a win.

Nevertheless, in 2011 a rematch was held, with Goldsborough fielding a new player: the long-haired and beer-bellied Gary Watson from Leeds. Gary was, however, not all that he seemed.

His beer belly was a cushion stuffed down his trousers, while his real identity was disguised by means of prosthetics that took five hours to apply – because Gary was, in fact, England player Michael Vaughan. Vaughan had made 5,719 runs in his Test career and the stunt was put together to publicise a drive to support grassroots cricket by NatWest bank.

In the end, Gary managed twenty-eight runs before being dismissed, which would have, had his real identity been known, been quite a scoop for Goldsborough's opponents.

It turned out to be quite difficult even for such a cricketer as Vaughan to play in prosthetics and make runs while waddling around with a cushion stuffed down his trousers!

RAIN AND WHAT ELSE
STOPPED PLAY?

The two most common causes for cricket matches being paused or suspended are rain and bad light. This might make you wonder how some parts of England are ever able to host entire matches. Nevertheless, they are not the only cause of interruptions. Matches have also been held up by an extraordinary range of mishaps, bizarre occurrences, wildlife, motor vehicles and even just people trying to make themselves a snack.

In November 2017 at Allan Border Field in Brisbane, play was dramatically brought to a stop on day three of a Sheffield Shield match between New South Wales and Queensland.

New South Wales were on their way to a resounding victory. They needed just eighteen runs, but suddenly a fire alarm began sounding in the Stuart Law grandstand.

The stand was evacuated and players had to leave the field immediately without being allowed to return to the dressing rooms. Meanwhile, officials began investigating the source of the apparent inferno while fire trucks were summoned to the ground.

Eventually, Aussie spin bowler Nathan Lyon confessed to being the culprit responsible for the thirty-minute break in play. He was guilty of the heinous crime of trying to make himself a piece of toast in the pavilion.

Lyon said his toast had popped up but it had not looked sufficiently brown. He therefore popped it back down again and forgot about it. He had overlooked the fact that the one thing guaranteed to set a smoke alarm off is a slightly over-toasted piece of toast.

'I wasn't happy so I put it back down,' Lyon recalled, 'and I got carried away watching the cricket ... There's a first for everything.'

In 2007, Lancashire were facing Kent in the County Championship at Old Trafford when the fire alarm went off in the pavilion. A fourth-wicket stand between Darren Stevens and Martin van Jaarsveld was interrupted by the emergency while two fire engines were called to the scene, where the cause of the alarm turned out to be a neglected pot of gravy that had begun to smoulder in the kitchen.

In South Africa in 1995, during a Currie Cup match at Paarl, an octopus barbecue temporarily halted play, but this time it wasn't burning food that had caused the stoppage.

Daryll Cullinan hit Roger Telemachus for six only for the ball to land in the barbecue, in which calamari was being prepared by a spectator. Play was then held up for ten minutes while umpires waited for the ball to cool down enough so it could be picked up again and wiped clean of grease.

Play then resumed, but the barbecue ultimately caused another delay, when Telemachus demonstrated that it was no longer possible to grip the by now octopus-grease-infused leather. The ball, therefore, had to be changed for a non-barbecued one.

The first recorded occasion that rain stopped play was in a match held at White Conduit Fields, Islington, London on 1 September 1718 between teams representing London and the Rochester Punch Club Society.

The Rochester team declared that heavy rain made it 'impossible to continue the game', but the London team did not seem to agree. The matter was taken to court and the Lord Chief Justice declared that the game should be completed.

London ended up winning by twenty-one runs and received £60 in prize money plus almost another £140 to cover the legal costs.

In 2007, an MCC university contest between Surrey and Leeds/Bradford University Centre of Cricketing Excellence was held up when a giant cigarette stopped play.

The Oval had hired a man to dress in a giant cigarette outfit to publicize the recently introduced ban on smoking in the ground. Unfortunately, the man inside the costume could not see very well. He therefore failed to heed all instructions and directions being conveyed to him and ended up wandering behind the bowler just as he was about to run in, lending further support to the argument that cigarettes are not good. In the end, a loudspeaker announcement had to be made to tell the enormous cigarette to sit down.

After play resumed at Lord's following an interruption because of a streaker running across the pitch, Richie Benaud quipped: 'There was a slight interruption there for athletics.'

Jonathan Agnew, on other hand, said: 'I've never got to the bottom of streaking.'

The fourth day of a 1995 Test match between England and the West Indies at Old Trafford was also interrupted, this time by both male and female streakers. It was also the same day that umpire Dickie Bird had lost his marbles and then had to crawl around on the pitch for several minutes trying to find them so he could record bowling deliveries. These were not, however, the first interruptions during this Test.

On day two, Bird had had to call for an early tea because of rain and for a premature end to the day's play because of poor light – all rather conventional. The previous day's play, however, had been stopped because of sunlight reflecting off a greenhouse adjacent to the ground. Only in cricket would a sporting fixture be delayed by a see-through structure many metres from the action itself.

A similar problem had been encountered in 1963 during a game between Essex and Derbyshire. On that occasion, the sun was dazzling everyone on the pitch as it reflected off the windshields of the players' cars, which were parked alongside the ground. Play was therefore suspended while the players all left the field, found their keys and proceeded to move their cars.

And in 1962–63, when England played New Zealand in Christchurch, play was stopped because the ground's recently installed new stand turned out to be made of aluminium. The effect was blinding when the sun shone on the its nice new shiny surface.

In June 2019 during a match between Sri Lanka and South Africa in the Cricket World Cup at the Riverside Ground, Chester-le-Street, County Durham, play was stopped by bees. The spectators were thankfully unaffected and thus able to sit and enjoy the spectacle of players and umpires throwing themselves to the ground, where they had to lie flat for several minutes as a swarm of bees swept over the batting crease.

Sri Lanka's and Australia's cricketers should have been used to such pitch invasions. It had happened when the two teams played each other in a one-day international in Johannesburg just two years earlier. Again players and umpires had to lie flat on the ground at the Wanderers ground while a swarm of bees did their worst.

On that occasion, attempts were made to get the bees to move on by use of sticks, a fire extinguisher, a bucket of Coca Cola, some honey and, finally – and most successfully – an actual beekeeper.

As far back as 1962, bees had held up play in a match between Oxford University and Worcestershire, while a 'very large' swarm also intervened when Lampeter CC played Bronwydd in 1988. A bee attack occurred at Asgiriya Stadium in Kandy in December 2007 during a match between Sri Lanka and England, and another in October 2008 during a Test match between India and Australia at the Feroz Shah Kotla Stadium, Delhi. A swarm during a match in India in 2019 not only forced play to stop but also resulted in five spectators being taken to hospital. It is not recorded whether these injuries resulted from bee stings, fire extinguishers going off, their being accidentally hit with buckets of Coca Cola or jars of honey, or their being barged aside by beekeepers trying to make their way on to the field.

Play was stopped on two occasions at Headingley Cricket Ground in the early 1960s by a dog called Brutus.

Brutus lived in a house overlooking the stadium and managed to gain entry during England's Ashes match in 1961 and again during their Test match against Pakistan in 1962. He ran around the field for a few minutes evading capture and exited via a gate at the Kirkstall Lane End.

Despite his repeated pitch invasions, Brutus became known as a lucky mascot for England. The team won in both the matches in which Brutus had attended, but in 1963, when they faced the West Indies, Brutus did not see fit to appear and England promptly lost the match.

A famous canine interruption occurred in the 1993 Test at Trent Bridge when Merv Hughes was about to bowl to Mark Lathwell. Before the first ball was bowled, a stray dog wandered in and stopped play. Hughes showed his softer side as he took charge of the situation by going down on all fours to talk to the dog, bristly face to bristly face.

The dog was removed and reportedly adopted and given the name Merv.

Peter, the Lord's cat, never stopped a game. Nevertheless, following his death on 5 November 1964, he became the only animal whose demise was listed in *Wisden*: 'Cat, Peter, whose ninth life ended on November 5, 1964, was a well-known cricket watcher at Lord's.'

Peter had been a regular from 1952 to the end of his life and would creep in to watch proceedings whenever the crowd was at its largest. Although he appeared in the course of television broadcasts from Lord's during this time, oddly there seems to be no photograph of Peter at the ground or elsewhere.

In August 1957, a mouse managed to hold up play between Kent and Hampshire. It ran on to the field, followed shortly thereafter by its owner, who had clearly been treating it to a day out to watch the cricket. He somehow managed to scoop the mouse up safely in his hat and play resumed. A Test match between England and Pakistan at Lord's was also held up as a result of a pitch invasion by a mouse in 1962.

Brian Johnston was commentating when a little black-and-white dachshund appeared on the pitch during a match at Headingley, and could not resist the opportunity for a quip. 'I can tell you at home that this dachshund is a fast bowler,' said Johnston, 'and the reason I know he's a fast bowler is because he's got four short-legs and his balls swing both ways.'

Play was stopped during Derbyshire's County Championship match against Gloucester in July 1957 by a hedgehog that wandered on to the field. The players tried to shoo the poor creature away but to no avail.

Eventually they worked out that they needed someone in possession of a large, thick pair of gloves to remove the prickly visitor. Luckily, Derbyshire's wicketkeeper George Dawkes was on hand and the hedgehog was thus escorted from the field.

In May 2011, a match between Hampshire Academy and South Wiltshire at the Rose Bowl cricket ground, Southampton, was suspended because a tiger had been spotted in a nearby field.

Firstly, a rumour had gone round the stadium that there was a big cat in the vicinity. Everyone remarked how interesting this news was before play carried on as normal. The police then turned up and informed all those assembled that tigers were in fact quite dangerous creatures and, in the circumstances, it would be best to clear the area in case of a pitch invasion by a man-eating beast.

Meanwhile, a police helicopter had located and was keeping a close eye on the creature while a team from nearby Marwell Zoo were arming themselves with tranquilizer darts as they prepared to go out and face the animal.

The tranquilizers proved to be unnecessary. A downdraft from the police helicopter suddenly blew the tiger over. Officers began to suspect that they might not have been dealing with a large, deadly predator after all. Further investigation revealed the tiger to be a stuffed toy (albeit one that looked quite realistic from a distance) and play resumed once more. Nevertheless, despite requests from the police, the owner of the life-size cuddly tiger did not come forward to reclaim their item or explain why they had left it in the middle of a Hampshire field.

Play in the June 2012 Ranji Trophy match between Delhi and Uttar Pradesh was halted when a small hatchback drove into the ground and, despite attempts from players and umpires to stop him, out on to the pitch at the Palam Air Force Ground.

The driver, Girish Sharma, said he had not encountered security on his way in and claimed he had got a bit lost. It was only once he was inside the ground that the security guards decided to take decisive action. They immediately closed the gates to stop him driving back out again.

Mr Sharma was then caught and handed over to the

police. After an inspection, the pitch was deemed not to have endured significant damage and the referee declared it playable. An official subsequently made a statement that security would be increased at the gate into the ground from the next day.

As we have established, play is most often disrupted by bad light or rain. It was therefore a surprise when good light stopped play at Old Trafford in September 2010.

The sun's glare was so strong on the second day of a match between Lancashire and Nottinghamshire that play had to be delayed. The sun shining was a particularly unusual reason for play to be suspended, as the match was being held in Manchester, an area normally renowned for its less than clement weather. Indeed, play had already been delayed because of rain that same day. Spectators had had to wait until 4 p.m. for the downpour to ease off and play to commence, only for it to be suspended again ninety minutes later because the sun was now reflecting too brightly off the Stretford End commentary-box roof.

Play was resumed once more but, after just a few more overs, the players had to go off yet again because play couldn't continue after 6 p.m.!

CLASSIC SCORECARDS

O ne of cricket's best scorecard entries of all time was written on 18 December 1979. The recorded event occurred at the WACA ground in Perth during a three-Test series between England and Australia. Mike Brearley won the toss and put his opponents into bat. Expectations were riding high. This was not just because of the rivalry between the two sides but also because both Graham Dilley and Peter Willey had been included in the England team, while the Australian team of course featured Dennis Lillee. Tantalizing comic possibilities also existed because of the presence of Willey in the England line-up facing off against Australia's Julien Wiener. The Test was also remembered for Dennis Lillee's controversial use of an aluminium bat.

Nevertheless it was Dilley, Willey and Lillee who would provide the match's legendary cricketing headline. The commentators looked forward to the various possibilities. Lillee being caught by Dilley after being bowled by Willey was considered the least likely outcome because of Dilley's lack of experience as a bowler at the time.

And then the dream came true. Lillee was unable to keep a ball down from Dilley and Willey went on to take the catch. Lillee had been caught by Willey with the ball being bowled by Dilley.

And thus the scorecard record of the dismissal went down into history and endless pub quiz questions: 'Lillee c Willey b Dilley'.

In June 1933, Middlesex played Somerset at Lord's. The Somerset team included twenty-eight-year-old Frank Lee and his thirty-one-year-old brother Jack. Middlesex had, however, been the home of the Lee family and indeed Frank had been born just a stone's throw away from Lord's. Thus the Middlesex team included yet another member of the Lee family: Frank and Jack's elder brother, Harry.

When Harry batted on the second day, he reached eighty-two before getting out to a ball bowled by his brother Jack and caught by his brother Frank. And thus the scorecard read: 'H. Lee c F. Lee b J. Lee 82.'

Ultimately, Middlesex won by eight wickets but Harry later wrote of his dismissal in the first innings: 'I do not believe that brothers had ever before behaved so unbrotherly in a first-class game.'

In 2017, Australian Glenn Maxwell became captain of the Indian Premier League team Kings XI Punjab. That year, the team's line-up included Sandeep Sharma and Mohit Sharma. They were due to play Mumbai, whose team coincidentally included Rohit Sharma and Karn Sharma. Maxwell then decided to make a change and brought in Ishant Sharma as well.

'We decided we didn't have enough Sharmas in the team,' Maxwell explained.

There were, then, five Sharmas over the two teams, thereby making the match 22.7 per cent Sharma. None of the Sharmas were related to one another, nor were they related to the other three players called Sharma playing in the IPL that year.

If three Lees or five Sharmas seem overwhelming enough, in July 2001 a Sunday school league match was held in Bradford between Yorkshire LPS and Amarmilan, with each team fielding nothing but players called Patel. Yes, there were twenty-two Patels in the match that day.

One of the scorers, who was (by complete coincidence) also called Patel, commented: 'I was shocked. Some players even had the same first four initials, so everyone's names had to be written in full.'

Even more surprisingly, rather than being a stunt, the event had happened entirely by accident. The LPS club secretary (Ishy Patel) said it was only because the team's regular wicketkeeper, who was not called Patel, had to go to London for work. Luckily, Patel was available instead.

Yorkshire LPS won by thirty-one runs and one can only presume that Patel was declared man of the match – if not men of the match.

One of the longest surname-only scorecard entries in first-class history occurred in November 1990. Kerala were playing Andhra in the Indira Priyadarshini Stadium, Visakhapatnam. Kerala's team included perhaps their greatest player, Karumanaseri Narayanaiyer Ananthapadmanabhan, as well as his elder brother Karumanaseri Narayanaiyer Balasubramaniam. When the Andhra captain Vankenna Chamundeswaranath came out to bat, he only scored two.

Nevertheless, the resulting scorecard entry was both extensive and magnificent: Chamundeswaranath c Balasubramaniam b Ananthapadmanabhan (at Visakhapatnam).

Sri Lanka is the world-beater when it comes to cricketers with extremely long names. Uda Walawwe Mahim Bandaralage Chanaka Asanga Welegedara played for Sri Lanka in 2007 and although more commonly known as Chanaka Welegedara, he is the record-holder for having more initials than anyone else to have played Test cricket.

Other impressively named Sri Lankan cricketers include: Mataramba Kanaththa Gamage Chamila Premanath Lakshitha (aka Chamila Garnage), who made his debut in 2002; left-arm wrist-spinner Paththamperuma Arachchige Don Lakshan Rangika Sandakan (Lakshan Sandakan); left-arm fast bowler Warnakulasuriya Patabendige Ushantha Joseph Chaminda Vaas (Chaminda Vaas); legendary spin bowler Herath Mudiyanselage Rangana Keerthi Bandara Herath (Rangana Herath); and left-handed batsman/right-arm medium-fast bowler Amunugama Rajapakse Rajakaruna Abeykoon Panditha Wasalamudiyanse Ralahamilage Rajitha Krishantha Bandara Amunugama (or ARRAPWRRKB Amunugama, or Rajitha Amunugama).

Sri Lanka does not, however, have a monopoly on long cricketing names. John Elicius Benedict Bernard Placid Quirk Carrington Dwyer played for Sussex between 1904 and 1909 and is a record-holder as the only English player to have had seven initials, although these were usually abbreviated to J. B. Dwyer.

The player with the longest name to have ever played first class cricket was Fiji's greatest cricketer, Ilikena Lasarusa Talebulamaineiilikenamainavaleniveivakabulaimainakulal-akebalau. He debuted against New Zealand in the 1947–48 season. Having to trot out his entire official name every time he was mentioned might have taken several overs, so instead his name was helpfully abbreviated to I. L. Bula, which is the Fijian for 'Life'. His full name, Talebulamaineiilikena-mainavaleniveivakabulaimainakulalakebalau, translates as 'Returned alive from Nankula Hospital at Lakeba Island in the Lau Group'.

In 1913, Derbyshire's line-up included not only bowler Fred Root but also the team's occasional wicketkeeper George Beet. On the third day of their match against Sussex at the County Ground, Derby in July 1913, Beet was on wicketkeeping duties while Root bowled to the Sussex captain Herbert Chaplin. Chaplin snicked the ball, Beet caught the catch behind the wicket and thus, for the first and only time in first-class cricket, the scorecard read: c Beet b Root.

In July 1870, Surrey were playing the MCC at the Oval. W. G. Grace caught a ball from Surrey's batsman James Southerton on the bounce. Southerton had played his stroke with his eyes closed. When he opened them and saw Grace holding the ball, he walked despite the fact that the bounce had been so evident that none of the umpires or other players, including Grace, had called him out.

Nevertheless, Southerton insisted on continuing on his

way back to the pavilion and declaring himself out. The scorecard was therefore duly entered as: 'J Southerton, retired thinking he was out, 0.'

A LACK OF MODERATION
IN ALL THINGS

Whether it's the lovely cakes and hot drinks available during the tea break or perhaps even the odd alcoholic beverage, cricket provides plentiful opportunity for overindulgence. Henry Blofeld, for example, said he would never forget the occasion when veteran commentator John Arlott turned up at Lord's for *Test Match Special* armed with two heavy briefcases.

Blofeld helped carry the two mysterious cases up to the commentary box. They were then carefully positioned on a table in the corner before Arlott opened the first to reveal six bottles of claret and two corkscrews. Arlott, it seems, always carried two corkscrews, his mantra being: 'If one of them breaks, you're buggered!' He then went on to open his second briefcase, which contained another five bottles of claret.

Once all eleven bottles were unpacked, Arlott intoned:

'With any good fortune, that little lot should see us through to the lunch interval.'

Aussie batsman David Boon was once reported to have drunk fifty-eight cans of beer during a flight from Australia to England. Thankfully the veteran Australian cricketer Ian Chappell was on hand to put things in perspective: 'In my day,' Chappell said, 'fifty-eight beers between London and Sydney would have virtually classified you as a teetotaller.'

In 2007, following a drunken escapade in the middle of the night, Andrew 'Freddie' Flintoff was stripped of his vice-captaincy of the England team for one match. He also picked up a brand-new nickname in the process.

England had just lost at Gros Islet, St Lucia, to New Zealand in their first match of the 2007 World Cup. In response to the defeat, Flintoff went on an eight-hour drinking spree with his teammates. When he finally got back to the luxury Rex St Lucian Hotel where he was staying, rather than going to bed to sleep it all off, he decided instead to brush past a security guard and set out to sea on board a pedalo.

Flintoff later revealed that he had set off on his pedalo excursion to visit and have a nightcap with Ian Botham, who he knew was on board one of the boats moored out across the bay. Flintoff tried a kayak first but couldn't find the oars and so instead attempted to charter the rough Caribbean Sea by pedalo. This was an ill-advised move and a member of the hotel staff had to drag him back to land before he drowned himself. He awoke the next morning still wet, with sand between his toes and stripped of his vice-captaincy. Flintoff expressed his contrition: 'I know that what I did on Friday night was completely wrong and I have to take full responsibility for it ... There can be no excuses on my part. I know I shouldn't have done what I did and I have to accept the punishment.'

But at least he got a new nickname out of the incident: Fredalo.

In December 2006, Flintoff was England captain for the Ashes series. The previous year, under Michael Vaughan, England had won the Ashes back for the first time in eighteen years. Vaughan was injured for the 2006–07 Ashes and so the captaincy was offered to Flintoff.

Unfortunately, things did not go well, and England were thumped 5–0 in the series. Following the final Test, Flintoff received more flak when he was seen out drinking with Ricky Ponting and Shane Warne.

He responded by saying he couldn't understand the criticism: 'We did exactly the same at the Oval last year when we took the Ashes away from them!'

The previous year, Flintoff had of course celebrated England's Ashes victory by going on a twenty-four-hour bender. Afterwards he said, 'I don't regret it, but I wish they hadn't put the pictures in the paper!'

The future umpire David Shepherd was a rather solid-looking figure even in his younger days when playing for Gloucestershire. When the Gloucestershire team were sent on a cross-country run one morning, Shepherd was soon left plodding along behind the others. And so when he spotted a milk float coming up behind him, as Dickie Bird described in his autobiography, he decided to use a bit of initiative.

Shepherd hopped on board and, as Bird put it, 'sat on the ledge, holding on for dear life, with the bottles tinkling merrily around him and his legs wobbling in the air. He was first back to the county ground at Bristol, and the other lads could not believe it when they huffed and puffed their way into the ground to see Shep there with a smirk of superiority on his face.'

Ian Healy said of Shane Warne that his 'idea of a balanced diet is a cheeseburger in each hand'.

A newspaper commented of Bangladesh captain Khaled Mahmud: 'His claim of being an all-rounder is clearly more a reflection of his physique than abilities in Test cricket.'

Mike Gatting, who played for England from 1977 to 1995, was renowned for sporting a fuller figure and enjoying a healthy appetite. On 4 June 1993, day two of the first Ashes Test at Old Trafford, Gatting was dismissed by Shane Warne. Warne's extraordinary delivery, later dubbed 'the ball of the century', arrived at Gatting before making a sharp left turn to clip the top of his off stump.

Graham Gooch, who was at the non-striker's end, described the expression on Gatting's face following the dismissal: 'He looked as though someone had just nicked his lunch'.

Gooch later also remarked: 'If it had been a cheese roll, it would never have got past him.'

Following the incident, cricket journalist Martin Johnson mused: 'How anyone can spin a ball the width of [Mike] Gatting boggles the mind.'

Both David Gower and Mike Gatting recalled an exchange that occurred during the 1984–85 series between England and India.

Gatting asked Gower, 'Should I get wider at cover, David?'

'No, mate,' interjected Chris Cowdrey. 'If you get any wider, you'll burst.'

Commentator Richie Benaud once remarked: 'Gatting at fine leg: that's a contradiction in terms.'

In 1988, Gatting was accused of having had young barmaid Louise Shipman in his hotel room during the first Test against West Indies at Trent Bridge. The English cricket authorities accepted Gatting's denial of being involved with Shipman but said that he should not have had her up in his room in the first place. Ian Botham, meanwhile, helpfully added: 'It couldn't have been Gatt. Anything he takes up to his room after nine o'clock, he eats.'

On another occasion, Botham discussed some of the complaints that had been levelled against his own behaviour: 'If I'd done a quarter of the things of which I'm accused, I'd be pickled in alcohol, I'd be a registered drug addict and would have sired half the children in the world's cricket-playing countries.'

In 2003, Martin Kelner reviewed the TV documentary *The Real Geoff Boycott*, which had been broadcast on Channel 4 and had created a rather disturbing mental image.

'The programme,' wrote Kelner, 'implied that "the powerful attraction exerted by this apparently charmless man" may have lain in his discovery of a kind of Yorkshire version of tantric sex. That is, he made love like he played cricket: slowly, methodically, but with the real possibility that he might stay in all day.'

Australian all-rounder Keith Miller was said to be the polar opposite to Don Bradman with regard to his carousing and enjoyment of life. Neville Cardus went so far as to refer to him as 'the Australian in excelsis', while John Arlott once said of him that he seemed 'busy living life in case he ran out of it'.

People wondered about the extent of the friendship between Princess Margaret and the dashing Keith Miller. When asked about their relationship, Miller commented: 'Put it this way, we had a lot of fun.'

There was certainly some indication that Miller knew his way around the royal residence surprisingly well. When the Australian team visited Buckingham Palace in 1953 and captain Lindsay Hassett was about to lead his men into the palace, Miller wandered off towards a distant building.

'Where are you going?' Hassett asked.

'It's okay, skipper,' replied Miller. 'There's another entrance here.'

Thank goodness Miller had 'had a lot of fun' with Princess Margaret, as there was less enjoyment to be had on the pitch that year. It was in 1953 that Australia lost the Ashes at home for the first time since the bodyline tour thirty years earlier.

Hampshire captain Colin Ingleby-Mackenzie was legendary for keeping late hours. He was seen on more than one occasion turning up for a match still wearing the dinner jacket he had been wearing the night before. Burning the candle at both ends did not, however, seem to hamper his performance. Following one all-night drinking session in 1958, for example, he managed to hit a hundred in just sixty-one minutes. When he was asked the secret of his side's success, he put it down to 'wine, women and song'.

In a later interview following Hampshire's winning the County Championship in 1961, he was asked if they would now continue to pursue the same philosophy. Ingleby-Mackenzie replied that they might consider giving up the singing.

One of Ingleby-Mackenzie's most famous moments came when an interviewer asked him what rules he had for team discipline.

'Well,' he said, 'everyone in bed in time for breakfast, I suppose!'

In Henry Blofeld's retelling of this quip, Ingleby-Mackenzie was asked if there was a curfew for his players when they stayed in hotels for away games. Ingleby-Mackenzie said he liked them to be in bed for half past nine. The interviewer responded by saying that sounded rather early.

'Not really,' said Ingleby-Mackenzie. 'The game starts at half past eleven.'

NICKNAMES

Cricket provides a fertile ground for nicknames given in honour or at the expense of many of its greatest figures. Or sometimes the names just arise by pure accident!

The England and Warwickshire left-arm spinner Ashley Giles has one of the most unusual nicknames in the game: the King of Spain. The name dates back to 2001, but did not involve any claim to the Spanish throne on Giles' part.

Instead, it resulted from an order of souvenir mugs for the Warwickshire club shop. These were designed to show Warwickshire's red-and-yellow insignia alongside an image of Ashley Giles, depicted after a triumphant ball. The words 'King of Spin' were to be printed in large letters on the front of the mug. Unfortunately, due to a typesetting error, when the mugs arrived at Edgbaston they were found to have the title 'King of Spain' next to Giles' portrait.

Inevitably, the name stuck, and ever since Ashley Giles has been known to cricket fans as the heir to King Felipe VI.

England all-rounder Andrew Flintoff has had many nicknames over the years but the most famous of all is, of course, 'Freddie'. He was first dubbed Freddie as a teenager by John Stanworth, captain of Lancashire's second XI. The joke was in reference to 'Fred Flintstone', even though no one has ever referred to the cartoon Bedrock inhabitant as Freddie. Flintoff's nickname has nevertheless served as the basis of various other names over the years, such as SuperFred and Mr InFredible.

There is just one problem. The fact that Andrew Flintoff's nickname 'Freddie' Flintoff sounds like a normal name has led to some confusion. At least one online list of incredible facts about Andrew Flintoff begins with the following: 'Many people do not realize that Andrew Flintoff and Freddie Flintoff are the same person.'

Perhaps Flintoff's two names indicate a Jekyll-and-Hyde-like situation. Andrew is the brilliant cricketer while Freddie is the persistent overindulger!

Mike Atherton was nicknamed 'the Cockroach' by the Australians in general and possibly by Steve Waugh in particular. The reason? He was so difficult to stamp out.

New Zealander Gavin Larsen was dubbed 'the Postman' by his teammates because, as the team's manager John Graham said, 'He always delivers.'

One of Merv Hughes' nicknames was 'Sumo', and crowds would chant this as he prepared to bowl. He was also known as 'the Fruit Fly'. Some people wondered why this name was thought to be appropriate until one day Allan Border explained that Hughes was Australia's greatest national pest.

Ian Botham has had several nicknames over the years. None of these seem particularly flattering, although you would presume the Lord Botham might tolerate some of them more than others. His physique gained him the nicknames 'Beefy' and 'Guy' (as in Guy the Gorilla), but as a youngster he was known as Bungalow. This turned out not to be because he was built like a bungalow but because his teammates thought he had nothing upstairs.

England's Chris Lewis gained the unfortunate nickname 'the Prat without a Hat' after spending time fielding during England's 1994 Test in Antigua. When he became concerned about the intense temperatures in the Caribbean, he asked teammate Devon Malcolm to shave his hair off for him. This, coupled with the fact that he didn't bother to put on a hat or apply any sunscreen, led to *the Sun* newspaper dubbing him 'the Prat without a Hat' and saying that Lewis 'baldly went where no other cricketer has gone before'. He had to miss his next match because he had to spend two days in bed suffering from sunstroke.

Sadly, this was not the worst example of poor decision-making by Lewis. In 2009, following a trip to St Lucia, he was stopped at Gatwick Airport by customs officers and found to be carrying £140,000 worth of cocaine into Britain in his cricket bag. He was convicted of smuggling and sentenced to thirteen years in prison.

New Zealand's Danny Morrison became known as 'the Duckman' in honour of the twenty-four ducks he achieved during his Test career. In 1996, a tie covered in ducks was made in his honour, while Morrison capitalized on his unfortunate soubriquet by marketing his own range of duck callers for hunters.

Kevin Pietersen had some fairly run-of-the-mill nicknames, such as 'Kev' and 'KP' (allegedly because some people thought he was nuts), and then of course there was the slightly more unusual 'FIGJAM'. No, this was not a reference to his hobby of making exotic fruit preserves but an epigrammatic way of saying: 'F*** I'm Good – Just Ask Me!'

The great West Indies fast bowler Michael Holding was famously nicknamed 'Whispering Death'. The 'whispering' was in reference to his smooth, silent approach to the wicket while the 'death' was the possible outcome when the ball flew from his hand.

In a quote variously attributed to John Arlott or possibly Alan Ross writing in *the Observer*, the New Zealander Bob Cunis' bowling was a bit like his name – 'neither one thing, nor the other'.

I DON'T THINK YOU
MEANT TO DO THAT ...

Some unkind souls might say that cricketers spend all their time trying to injure themselves or each other on the pitch. But that's not true at all. They're quite capable of injuring themselves off the pitch, as well.

In 1965, Ted Dexter was captain of Sussex and had been captain of England, but his playing career was brought to a premature end when he managed to run himself over with his own car.

When Dexter's Jaguar ran out of petrol on the Great West Road in West London, he decided that rather than wait for any breakdown help he would push the vehicle to the next garage. Unfortunately, this attempt to propel the car by manpower alone did not go smoothly and the vehicle ran out of control and ended up pinning Dexter to a warehouse door. Dexter's right leg was broken in the process, and he was left, as the writer Matthew Engel put it, 'with blood pouring out of his leg while other drivers rushed by'.

In 1982, England's Derek Pringle managed to injure himself while sitting at a desk trying to sort out complimentary tickets for some friends for the forthcoming Test match at Headingley.

As he sat engaged in the strenuous activity of attempting to arrange the tickets, he leaned back in his chair. The chair then collapsed beneath him and deposited him on the floor. This caused Pringle's back to spasm between the shoulder blades. Pringle did not want to disturb the team's physiotherapist so late at night, so he tried to cure the problem himself by sleeping on a mattress on the floor. Unfortunately, in so doing, he managed to make his back even worse and his withdrawal from the Test became inevitable.

Pringle's England teammates, however, did not seem to take his injury entirely seriously. Despite having been spared a midnight emergency, the team's physio now claimed that Pringle had injured himself 'writing letters'.

'The Machiavellian little man told the press I'd done my back in writing a letter,' complained Pringle. 'Presumably his attempt to toughen me up with some cod psychology.'

In 1921, Arthur Dolphin was playing for Yorkshire against Middlesex in a match at Lord's. Yorkshire not only lost the match but during its course Dolphin also managed to badly injure himself.

He did not suffer his injury on the pitch but in the dressing room. He had been sitting on a chair and at one point reached out a hand to get his clothes. Sadly, this caused him to lose his balance, fall and break his wrist. The injury was so bad he was ruled out for the rest of the season.

Former England captain Tony Greig was 6 ft 6 in, which made him prone to bumps and bruises from low door frames and ceilings. Greig also once managed to injure himself in an even more creative way when he stooped to look in a hotel bathroom mirror while shaving. He cricked his neck in the process and the accident left him unable to play in a forthcoming Test match.

Tony Greig's younger brother Ian played two Tests for England in 1982. The following year, he demonstrated why he was unlikely to make a living as a cat burglar.

Arriving home after the first day of a County Championship match with Kent in June 1983, he inserted his front-door key to let himself back into his home only for the key to snap in half. Greig then noticed an open window to one of the upstairs rooms. He decided to try to climb up the side of the house. Encouragingly, he managed to climb 18 ft up the wall. Less encouragingly, he didn't make it through the open window and instead fell to the ground and broke his ankle.

This was not the only instance of Greig being seemingly accident prone. A few years later, he injured his finger during a Surrey match and went to have it X-rayed. This revealed his finger was broken but then, just to make things even worse, Greig bashed his head on the X-ray machine as he got up. He required stitches as a result, although thankfully the X-ray machine was undamaged.

Chris Old was Botham's batting partner during the historic fightback against Australia in 1981. Old managed to put himself out of another Test match when he sneezed so violently that he damaged his ribs and left himself unable to play.

At the start of the 2006–07 season, Australia's opening batsman Matthew Hayden broke a finger taking a catch in a Sheffield Shield match against Tasmania in Brisbane. Hayden was thus temporarily out of the game. So, in an attempt to keep fit during the time he couldn't play, he took up jogging.

Just a week after breaking his finger, he was out doing a circuit round his neighbourhood when a dog saw him trotting past and decided that this sort of behaviour was not to be tolerated. The dog then proceeded to launch himself at Hayden's leg.

'It was a vicious attack,' Hayden said afterwards. 'I was just out for a leisurely run. You are always a bit shocked by that sort of thing, but I was more disappointed than anything. It just hasn't been my week.'

New Zealander Trevor Franklin had already broken his thumb during his team's 1986 tour, but things got considerably worse on the journey home.

Franklin was run down at London's Gatwick Airport by a motorized luggage trolley. The accident shattered Franklin's leg in multiple places and left him out of the game for eighteen months. Even when he returned, he was never again able to run at full speed. He nevertheless made a hundred during the 1990 Lord's Test but had his forearm broken when he faced David Lawrence in 1991–92.

Don Topley played for Essex for ten years but managed to injure himself during one off season – and not as a result of cricket practice.

During the colder months, Topley worked as a postman. On one occasion before the start of the new season, he tried to push a letter through a particularly tight letterbox. The spring-loaded flap snapped back on his fingers, causing significant damage and putting him out of action.

Sometimes cricketers can show real versatility by injuring themselves while playing a completely different sport.

Shortly before England's second Test against India in 2018, fast bowler James Anderson went for a round of golf with his teammate Stuart Broad at the Stoke Park course in Buckinghamshire. There, Anderson miscued a shot, which rebounded off a tree root and flew straight back into his face. Even more unluckily for Jimmy, Broad filmed the whole thing and posted it on Instagram.

It was during a 1967–68 tour of the West Indies that England spin bowler Fred Titmus suffered a truly grizzly accident.

Shortly before the third Test in Barbados, Titmus decided to go on a boat trip from Sandy Lane Bay, Barbados. While having a dip in the water, his left foot came into contact with the boat's propeller. Two of his toes were sliced off immediately, and two more were left hanging to his foot by threads. He was carried to a car by Denis Compton and Brian Johnston and was operated on by a Canadian specialist who was staying in the area at the time. It was assumed that he was unlikely to ever play again.

Titmus received just £90 compensation from the MCC's insurance. Possibly this miserliness inspired a swift return to the game for Titmus, who was back playing for Middlesex just ten weeks after the loss of 40 per cent of his toes. He made a stunning comeback and went on to play for nearly fifteen more years.

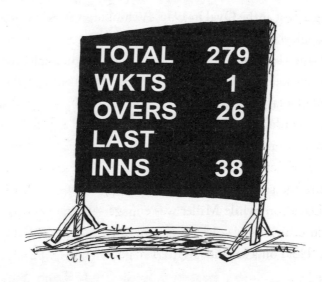

CAUGHT BEHIND

I t's unfortunate that cricketing sportswear is traditionally white, particularly in view of some of the trouser-related misfortunes that occur in the game.

During a Test at the Oval in 1956, Australian wicketkeeper Gil Langley squatted down only to hear a tearing sound from somewhere behind and slightly below. Sure enough, the somewhat burly Langley had just ripped his pants open in front of a large crowd.

As recorded in a famous photo of the event, his teammate Keith Miller was on hand with a safety pin. Miller instructed Langley to bend over and proceeded to secure the seat of his pants with the pin. According to Alan Davidson, while Miller was engaged in this delicate procedure, an Aussie voice from somewhere across the field yelled: 'Hold on a second, Keith! I've got a nappy!'

Sherlock Holmes author Arthur Conan Doyle was a keen amateur cricketer. In 1904, he was batting in a game when he suffered an accident that does not befall many players.

During the course of his innings, Conan Doyle suddenly burst into flames at the crease. Following a Holmesian investigation into the event, it was concluded that the ball had hit Conan Doyle on the thigh. The impact of this had been sufficient to ignite a small tin of matches that he was carrying in his pocket, and this had in turn set his trousers on fire.

This was, therefore, one of the rare occasions when a commentator could have described a batsman as quite literally 'being on fire' today.

Graeme Swann has never revealed the name of the teammate who suffered a particularly unfortunate experience in the middle of a county match. The player, Swann recalled, must have consumed 'a dodgy prawn' the night before his appearance. And so, while on the field, he thought he would 'let some trapped wind go'.

Unfortunately, what he had felt was not trapped wind and he ended up, in Swann's eloquent words, 'shitting his pants'.

'I must admit to chuckling quite hard at that one,' said Swann. 'It's the way he took it, as well. He just said, "Oh no, I've shat my pants!", turned around and legged it off the field.'

Indian cricketer Sachin Tendulkar was a prankster behind the scenes. In 2002, before India's ODI game against England at Cuttack, he recruited his teammate Hemang Badani to have a bit of fun at fast bowler Javagal Srinath's expense.

Despite his experience and illustrious career, Srinath was nervous before the England match and so, for the laudable reason of trying to distract him from his worrying, Badani was instructed to swap Srinath's trousers and replace them with a pair of Tendulkar's. The difference in leg length should have been obvious. Srinath was well over 6 ft tall and Tendulkar was only around 5 ft 5 in. Nevertheless, as Badani recalled: 'Srinath being Srinath, [he] doesn't even care. He finishes his practice, gets back to the dressing room, puts his trousers on, gets on the field, bowls the first ball, and there are people laughing on the field. The Indian side is laughing on the field, and little does he realize what's happened.'

Eventually, somebody called and remarked on the unusually short length of Srinath's trousers. Only then did he notice that he was at short leg, so to speak, and went to change into a pair more suited to his personal requirements.

According to Badani, Srinath then 'changed his trousers, went back in and he bowled a brilliant spell'.

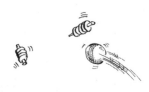

In July 2020 at Old Trafford, Ben Stokes reduced England captain Joe Root to tears of laughter when he took to the field sporting a very unfortunate brown stain on the seat of his trousers. Stokes offered the excuse that he must have sat in some coffee. Why he did this is unclear, unless his backside had been feeling a bit drowsy.

Nevertheless, other commentators on Twitter suspected the worst. Sports presenter Tim Coombs suggested that the stain had resulted from 'enforcing the follow through' and decorated his message with a particular emoji just in case anyone missed the point.

Gary Lineker, meanwhile, commented succinctly, 'Shit happens', to which the BBC's *Test Match Special* team replied in reference to Lineker's similar accident at the 1990 World Cup: 'Don't worry @GaryLineker you're now not the only one to have an "accident" on the pitch.'

GOING TO EXTREMES

Cricket is the world's oldest team sport as well as possibly being the one that takes longest to play. It is no surprise, therefore, that many of those associated with the sport have been inspired to go further than others, both in aspects of the game and elsewhere in life.

In his book *Fred: Portrait of a Fast Bowler*, John Arlott relates a story of a match in which Fred Trueman faced left-arm bowler Peter Sainsbury.

Time was beginning to run short so Sainsbury began trying to tempt Trueman into an injudicious stroke. Sainsbury 'tossed his slow left arm higher and higher' while Trueman 'resolutely abjuring his big swing, pushed forward with puritanical rectitude'.

After this had gone on for a while, with Sainsbury raising the curve more and more, Trueman turned to the wicketkeeper and said: 'My word! He chucks it up, this cock, doesn't he? I'm all right when his bloody arm comes over, but I'm out of form by the time the bloody ball gets here!'

In a slightly unexpected collision of worlds, Fred Trueman's daughter Rebecca married Hollywood star Raquel Welch's son Damon in June 1990. Sadly, the marriage did not last very long, and after just two years it was all over. Trueman nevertheless saw some humour in the situation when he commented that his daughter's marriage had lasted less time than it took him to complete his run-up.

Peter Pan author J. M. Barrie was a lover of cricket but felt his bowling was particularly slow. 'I bowl so slowly,' he once claimed, 'that if I don't like a ball I can run after it and bring it back.'

In the 1960s, Kent's Alan Brown was once denied an LBW appeal against Lancashire batsman Harry Pilling, who was just 5 ft 3 in tall.

Brown complained: 'Too high?! If the ball had hit his head it would have hit the bloody wickets!'

After a batsman deflected him between pad and leg stump, and made an on-side push and scored four to third man off the outside of the bat, Fred Trueman famously informed him: 'You've got more bloody edges than a broken piss pot.'

In his playing days, Surrey's Robin Jackman was known for his habit of appealing repeatedly and somewhat overdramatically. Henry Blofeld dubbed him 'the loudest appealer I can remember' while cricket writer Alan Gibson called Jackman the 'Shoreditch Sparrow', despite the fact he was neither from Shoreditch nor a sparrow.

Ian Botham was rather less eloquent and more to the point in his assessment of matters: 'When I first played against him I wanted to knock his head off because he really antagonized me. I thought, you arrogant, strutting gnome!'

Henry Blofeld described Lancashire and England wicketkeeper George Duckworth as the loudest appealer he had known. Blofeld recalled Lancashire playing Cambridge University on Fenner's Cambridge University Cricket Ground. If Duckworth unleashed one of his booming appeals, five batsmen were then given out over the road on Parker's Piece, where various other games were taking place.

Umpire Bill Reeve once said to George Macaulay, who played for Yorkshire and England between the wars: 'There's only one man made more appeals than you, George, and that was Dr Barnardo.'

LET'S NOT CALL THEM FLUKES

The game of cricket has throughout its history provided many unbelievable moments and strokes of luck. But as any of the players involved would surely tell you, these were all in fact completely intentional!

The longest six ever hit was by South African Jimmy Sinclair at the Old Wanderers ground, Johannesburg. It will be a difficult record to beat, as it ended up travelling 556 miles.

Sinclair was a tall, hard-hitting batsman but this wasn't the only thing that helped him achieve the record. A railway line passed close by one side of the ground. And so, when Sinclair hit the ball, it flew straight out of the ground and landed in a coal truck sitting on the tracks nearby. The ball could not be retrieved before the train moved on and it was thus carried all the way across the country to the coast and Port Elizabeth. But, despite all this, it still only scored six.

The ball was eventually recovered at its destination and sent back to the Wanderers ground where it was put on display for many years at the clubhouse. Hopefully play did not have to be suspended until its return.

On 15 January 1894, the *Pall Mall Gazette* reported a story about a game in Bunbury, Australia, between a team from Victoria and a scratch XI from the neighbourhood in Western Australia.

The Victorian team went in to bat and the very first ball that was struck flew into a tall jarrah tree growing inside the ground. And that is where it remained, as it had become lodged between the tree's branches. The Western Australians claimed that it was a lost ball but the umpire decided that, as it was still clearly in view (albeit stuck in a tree), it was not lost but still in play.

The Western Australia team now had to figure out how to get the ball back. They tried unsuccessfully to find an axe before being forced to resort to the next best thing – a rifle. After several attempts, they managed to shoot the ball out of the tree successfully. How many shots were necessary is not recorded because in the meantime their opponents from Victoria had put on 286 runs.

Theoretically, this was a world record for the most runs made off a single delivery. According to the story, the Victorians then declared and won the match with the shortest innings of all time.

When England faced South Africa at Durban in 1939, the match began on 3 March but didn't end until 14 March. The game had gone on for an incredible nine days of play spread over twelve days. It was the longest cricket match ever and was unsurprisingly known as the Timeless Test.

While the length of the match was extraordinary, the result was perhaps less so. It ended in a draw!

In previous centuries, several cricket matches were held between teams of one-legged and one-armed men. In 1766, 1796, 1841 and 1848, matches were held between teams of veterans of the British navy, who were now Greenwich pensioners. Bowling had to be underarm and the overs consisted of no more than four deliveries.

According to one account, during the 1796 match, one of the one-legged cricketers suffered a problem that doesn't happen very often in modern cricket. While he was making a run, his wooden leg dropped off. The detached appendage was then fielded in an attempt to stump the player.

One of the most famous stories about W. G. Grace is believed to have occurred during the 1896 Test against

Australia. Grace took to the crease and faced a ball bowled by Ernest Jones.

According to an account by Sir Pelham Warner, this first ball of England's first innings was very short and very fast and – unbelievably – it seemed to actually pass through Grace's beard. Warner described how wicketkeeper J. J. Kelly 'lost sight of it in Grace's beard and it went to the sight screen'.

Grace remonstrated about Jones' delivery, eliciting the immortal response from the bowler: 'Sorry, doctor! She slipped!'

Lord Harris wrote of the same incident but said that the ball had also touched the top of Grace's bat handle. C. B. Fry, in his autobiography, said that he had been playing for Lord Sheffield's XI when the event occurred at Sheffield Park near Horsted Keynes. After the ball had passed through his vast beard, Grace had said, 'What the hell are you at, Jonah?' or perhaps 'What, what, what?' And then at this point Jones responded by saying, 'Sorry, doctor! She slipped!'

On 30 August 1948 during a match at Lord's, Middlesex's spinner Jack Young bowled to Warwickshire's New Zealand-born batsman Martin Donnelly. As Donnelly

leaned forward, the ball pitched on his toe. It then flew up over the stumps and over Middlesex's wicketkeeper Dick Spooner only to then land in a footprint left by Middlesex's Laurie Gray. From here it bounced back again straight into the wicket.

The fielders appealed, although not with any particular confidence. Nevertheless, the umpire had to nod in agreement and Donnelly had to depart the crease, presumably wondering what on earth had just happened.

CRICKETERS WITH OTHER INTERESTS

Cricket is one of the most all-consuming of sports. Nevertheless, some of its practitioners have found time to pursue other careers and interests. Presumably, however, batting and bowling never strayed very far from their minds.

As well as being a pioneer of cricket and the first superstar of the game, W. G. Grace was also, of course, a qualified doctor of medicine. His priorities, however, often seemed to lie with his sporting interests rather than his duty of care.

A patient once came to his surgery and asked, 'Is Dr Grace in?'

The reply came, 'Of course he's in. He's been batting ever since lunchtime on Tuesday.'

While on a tour of Australia, the England team including Fred Trueman and the already ordained David Sheppard were presented to the Bishop of Perth. Trueman turned to Sheppard and remarked, 'I suppose he's your senior pro.'

In his capacity as doctor, W. G. Grace was once visited by a chimneysweep who arrived demanding a tonic. Grace replied that what the man needed was exercise rather than medicine. Grace then called to his maid to fetch his boxing gloves, at which point his patient decided to run away as fast as he could, crying as he went, 'The great big bastard wants to fight me!'

According to legend, Denis Compton was rather slovenly in dealing with the mail sent to him. In time, he filled a suitcase with unopened items of post, which he eventually handed to sports journalist Reg Hayter. Hayter worked through the envelopes and found among them a letter to Compton from the *News of the World* offering him £2,000 a year to write a column. Hayter rummaged further and found another letter from the paper, dated later and more sharply worded to inform Compton that, as he hadn't bothered replying, the offer was now being withdrawn.

Hayter decided Compton needed looking after and

introduced him to Bagenal Harvey, a businessman, who put him in touch with an advertising agency. The ad agency handled the marketing of Brylcreem hair product and Compton went on to make a fortune as the face of their brand.

In his book *Tuffers' Cricket Tales*, Phil Tufnell recalls a story concerning England spin bowler Phil Edmonds.

Edmonds had various business interests and continued to deal with these even during the course of matches in which he was playing for England. Edmonds would hold meetings at Lord's and get the lunch lady to send food and wine for him and his clients in the dining room. In the days of brick-like mobile phones, Edmonds even walked out on to the pitch and handed his phone to one of the umpires. Edmonds instructed the umpire, 'I'm expecting a call. Just give me a shout when it comes through.'

Colin Ingleby-Mackenzie was obsessed with betting and horse racing. Some even believed that he would sometimes deliberately miss a match if it clashed with an important race meeting. Whether this was true or not, he certainly managed to persuade at least one umpire to bring a radio out on to the field during a match so he could keep one ear on what was happening with the horse racing.

W. G. Grace was once setting off to play for Gloucestershire when an anxious mother tackled him, pleading, 'Dr Grace! I think my twins have measles. Can you come?'

'Not just now,' replied Grace, heading out of the door with his cricket kit. 'But contact me at the ground if their temperatures reach two-hundred and ten for two.'

BARMY ARMIES

Cricket attracts some of the greatest and most loyal fans in the world. They live for the game and devote their free time to following their teams around the world. Some might think they just want an excuse to get away from their families but cricket represents much more than that to them. It also provides an opportunity to travel to distant countries and shout abuse at opposing players.

The legendary writer and presenter Denis Norden commented on the realities that may hit a true cricket obsessive when autumn comes: 'It's a funny kind of month, October. For the really keen cricket fan, it's when you discover that your wife left you in May.'

According to a news report in August 1981, Mildred Rowley, a nurse from Wolverhampton, had just been granted a divorce from her husband after seventeen years of marriage. The reason for the split was because Mr Rowley's 'obsession with cricket constituted unreasonable behaviour'.

According to Mrs Rowley, cricket was not just a hobby for her husband but a total obsession. 'I had had just enough of it,' she commented.

For his part, Mr Rowley told the press, 'I don't blame Mildred for what she has done. I told her from the beginning cricket would always come first, but she did not believe me. I just can't exist without cricket.'

The divorce was granted despite the fact that Mr Rowley did not attend the hearing at Wolverhampton Divorce Court in person, as he was in Australia with Stourbridge Cricket Club at the time.

In 1950, the England team travelled to Australia by boat and disembarked at Sydney Harbour. As the young fast bowler John Warr stepped on to Australian soil, he was hailed by one of the wharf-side labourers working nearby, who greeted him with a memorable piece of imagery: 'Hey, Warr, you've got as much chance of taking a Test wicket on this tour as I have of pushing a pound of butter up a parrot's arse with a hot needle!'

In January 1983, Australian fans smuggled a piglet into the Gabba in Brisbane. After Botham was dismissed, the animal was released on to the pitch with 'BOTHAM' written on one of his sides and 'HEMMINGS' on the other. The reason for this was that, at the time, both England's Ian Botham and Eddie Hemmings favoured a slightly curvaceous body image.

The question of how the fans had managed to get the pig into the ground remained. The piglet handler later explained that he had smuggled his pink porcine friend into the ground by putting an apple in its mouth and telling the security guards that he had brought it for his lunch.

The Aussie opener Matthew Hayden branched out and published *The Matthew Hayden Cookbook* **in 2004, prompting at least one English fan to shout at him: 'You're shit, Hayden, and so is your chicken casserole!'**

An Aussie fan once called out a timeless line to England spinner Phil Tufnell: "Ey, Tufnell! Can I borrow your brain? I'm building an idiot!'

Bodyline-era England captain Douglas Jardine was fielding during a Test in Australia when he was spotted angrily trying to swat away some persistent flies.

A voice yelled out from among the Australia supporters: 'Leave our flies alone, Jardine! They're the only friends you've got here!'

Even Harold Larwood, an England bowler in the 1920s and 1930s, once commented: 'A cricket tour in Australia would be the most delightful period in your life … if you were deaf.'

A new batsman walks out to the crease for his first innings but plays so badly that after a few minutes the crowd are beginning to slow-hand-clap him and shout abuse at his poor performance. Soon after the batsman is given out, by which time the barracking from the fans has intensified and he is being pelted with rotten eggs and fruit as he returns to the pavilion.

'Blimey,' says the batsman when he gets back to the dressing room. 'They don't seem to like that umpire very much, do they?'

A young boy is so crazy about cricket his parents send him to a psychiatrist.

'All I ever do is dream about playing at Lords,' says the boy.

'Really?' says the psychiatrist. 'Don't you ever dream about girls?'

The boy replies, 'What!? And lose my turn to bat?'

One classic cricket anthem concerns Middlesex's Fred Titmus. The Birkenhead, Merseyside band Half Man Half Biscuit released their song 'F***in' 'Ell It's Fred Titmus' in 1985 on their first album, *Back in the DHSS*.

Nigel Blackwell's song was described by *The Rough Guide to Cult Pop* as 'the funniest song ever written about an England and Middlesex cricketer', and was suggested to *Test Match Special* in response to an invitation to listeners to choose their favourite cricketing songs.

Sadly, the lyrics of the song do not go into great detail about Titmus' career with Middlesex or England, or even the loss of four of his toes in a motorboat incident in Barbados. Instead they describe encounters with the by-then retired cricketer in various mundane settings, all of which climax with passers-by exclaiming, 'F***in' 'ell, it's Fred Titmus!'

Two women have husbands who are total cricket obsessives.

'How's your husband?' asks one.

'His cricket bat is giving him a lot of pain,' says the other.

'Oh no!' says the first. 'But how is his bat causing him pain?'

'I hit him over the head with it,' says the second.

It's the first day of an Ashes Test match. The stands are absolutely packed. A man notices the seat in front of him is the only empty one in the entire ground. He asks the man sitting next to the empty seat why he is alone.

'It's a sad story,' says the man. 'My wife and I got these tickets months ago and had been planning to come to this match together, but she died.'

'Oh no', says the first man. 'But couldn't you have asked a friend or relative to come with you instead?'

'I would have done,' says the bereaved man, 'but they're all at her funeral.'

TROUBLE ABROAD

Travelling abroad for cricketing purposes can lead to all manner of problems and confusion. Some of them even happen before touchdown.

For example, Alec Stewart was on his first Australian tour with England. When the team's flight was about to land in Perth, Stewart saw his teammate Darren Gough looking out of the window, while musing, 'It's amazing how low the planes get when we're coming into land, isn't it?'

Stewart also recalled how when England played in the Pakistan and India World Cup in 1996, he and Jack Russell had gone to extreme lengths to avoid Delhi belly. Stewart said he had bought 'a cricket case full of Tesco grub before we flew out'.

During his time in India and Pakistan, Stewart said he ate the same meal for forty-three days on the run. He claimed he had 'chicken breasts, mashed potatoes and broccoli every day'. Stewart said he didn't do curry in England so he wasn't going to do it in India or Pakistan either.

When he arrived back in England, his wife thought she would welcome him back with his favourite dinner and thus presented him with a lovely plate of chicken breast, mashed potato and broccoli.

Don Mosey once said of one of England's greatest batsmen: 'Boycott, somewhat a creature of habit, likes exactly the sort of food he himself prefers.'

The England team once stopped for a couple of nights in Aden, Yemen, while en route to Australia. During their brief stay, they were invited to attend a party at which one of their hosts pointed out a local Sheikh.

'He's got one-hundred and ninety-six wives,' said the host.

'Has he?' said Fred Trueman. 'Does he know that with another four he could have a new ball?'

During a trip to St Moritz in Switzerland, former England captain David Gower endured a mishap involving a 1990

Opel Vectra hire car and a frozen lake. In his defence, and possibly on his insurance claim form as well, Gower alleged that the ice on Lake St Moritz was a foot thick. It was so strong that he had recently been able to ride across it in a horse-drawn sled. Clearly the ice would hold even if someone was stupid enough to drive a car over it in the middle of the night. And that, of course, was exactly what Gower proceeded to do. And indeed the ice did hold. At least at first.

Problems only began to arise after Gower had been driving around on the frozen lake for, as he put it, 'a good hour or so'. He then decided to go back to his hotel. Unfortunately, Gower then discovered that his car's 'navigational thing' was wrong, although, in fairness, it might have got confused after spinning round on an icy expanse for some time in the middle of the night. It was at this point that Gower made what he described as his fatal error. This mistake taught him an important lesson about frozen lakes. Sadly, it was a lesson he learned slightly too late.

It turned out that the ice was thinner on points where water flowed in and out of the lake than it was elsewhere. Gower discovered this fact when he noticed some approaching grey ice and braked hard to avoid going over it. Unfortunately, this action caused him to stop right in the middle of it instead.

A quick glance out of the car window showed that the car was now a few inches below the main level of the ice. Gower tried to reverse back out of the hole he had just created but without success. Eventually he and his companions had to abandon the car, trudge across the ice and walk back up the hill to their hotel.

The next morning, Gower rang the hotel manager to ask a small favour.

'I have a slight problem,' Gower said. 'Could you do something for me and just see if there's a car on the lake?'

The manager phoned back ten minutes later and said, 'Mr Gower, there is no car on the lake.'

The ever-optimistic Gower thought that this sounded like good news. Maybe someone had stolen the car. Or perhaps someone else had moved it. The Swiss were, after all, a very efficient people. Maybe someone had taken the car, driven it off the lake, up the hill and popped it back in the hotel car park ready for him.

None of these options turned out to be the case. The car remained just where he'd left it but slightly lower down, out of view and now filled with water.

'The last I'd seen of it,' said Gower, possibly trying to rectify the situation with an impromptu advertisement for the Opel Vectra, 'it was shimmering in the moonlight looking quite glamorous for a mid-range hire car from Budget.'

David Gower's sinking Opel Vectra was not perhaps the most surprising sight a cricketer has ever unleashed while staying at a hotel.

When Derek Randall appeared on *Desert Island Discs*, he chose a nice warm bath as his luxury item. And indeed Randall must really enjoy a lovely soak in the tub because on one occasion after a day's play at the Adelaide Oval, he returned to his hotel and began running a bath for himself.

He proceeded to strip his clothes off so he was ready, but then decided to pop out of his room wearing only a towel to have a nice cup of tea with his teammates Ian Botham and Allan Lamb.

When Randall finally returned to his room, he reached in his pocket for his key only to discover he was dressed in a towel and therefore had neither pockets nor key. He then went down to the hotel reception to ask if they had a spare key available. He arrived in the lobby to discover various other guests running out of the restaurant soaked after it had mysteriously started raining indoors.

Randall approached the reception desk, still stark naked apart from his towel, and enquired what was going on.

'Well,' said the receptionist, 'some stupid c*** has left their bath running and flooded the dining room.'

THE TRAPPINGS
OF SUCCESS

Over the years, many of cricket's greatest figures have received rewards and honours for their contributions to the sport. But this being the world of cricket, respect and reverence don't always sit easily together!

In 1993, possibly Australia's greatest all-rounder Keith Miller was delighted when the MCC commissioned a portrait of him to be painted in oils and hung in the Long Room at Lord's. He complained, however, that despite his many years captaining New South Wales, the Sydney Cricket Ground 'haven't even named a gents' urinal after me!'

A statue of Dickie Bird was unveiled in the great umpire's hometown of Barnsley. The statue depicted Bird sticking his finger up as though giving a player out. Unfortunately, the extended finger was irresistible to passers-by, who delighted in hanging all manner of items from it. These included everything from pumpkins and chip boxes to condoms, bras and pants. Dickie Bird himself was occasionally seen having to reach up to remove items from his own statue's extended digit.

Eventually the local council had to take action to stop the ongoing abuse of Dickie Bird's finger. The statue was raised up on a higher plinth to make it a little more difficult for revellers to hang things on it – particularly if they were a bit worse for wear.

The Australian leg-spinner Arthur Mailey told a story of how he and his teammates were invited to the royal box after play at Lord's in 1923.

While being introduced to a female member of the Royal Family, Mailey told her, 'I'm a little stiff from bowling.'

'Oh,' she replied, 'is that where you are from? I was wondering.'

Keith Miller was a hero of the Royal Australian Air Force and flew numerous missions over Europe during the Second World War, but his commanding officer was less impressed with some of his other behaviour and informed him that he was an 'utter disgrace to the air force'.

The pair met again eight years after the war ended when Miller was part of the Australian team that toured England in 1953. During the visit, Miller made a trip to Royal Ascot and came dressed for the part in a top hat and tails, and driving a shiny Rolls-Royce. The attendant in the car park turned out to be none other than his old CO.

'Ah, my good fellow,' said Miller, pretending not to recognize him. 'Park my Rolls in the shade, will you? That's a good chap!'

On 4 July 1981, Her Majesty the Queen and Prince Philip visited Lord's on the third day of a Test between England and Australia. During the tea interval, the royal couple were introduced to the teams. The Australians assembled in line to greet them and were presented one by one by their captain Kim Hughes. Denis Lillee had on a previous occasion greeted Her Majesty with a cheerful 'G'day, Queen' before asking for a royal autograph. Luckily this time there were no similar transgressions of protocol until the royals were introduced to Rodney Hogg. After they had passed by and while the Queen was still well within earshot, Hogg remarked to his teammates: 'Jeez, she hasn't

got bad legs for an old sheila, has she?!'

This was of course a good old Aussie compliment, but hopefully Her Majesty had not been in earshot two years earlier when the team had visited Buckingham Palace. Manager David Richards had given his men strict instruction not to swear while they were at the palace, at which point Hogg had piped up to enquire: 'Does that mean we can't say "f***" in front of the Queen?!'

STILL AT THE CREASE

In August 2019, West Indies fast bowler Cecil Wright announced he would be retiring from the game, with his last match being on 7 September. Wright was aged eighty-five and he had had a sixty-year career. Reports of the octogenarian player's retirement didn't even put his description of himself as a fast bowler in quotation marks. Unlike many other sports, in cricket some continue to play even to the most advanced ages. And in some cases, players might even improve with time.

When India toured Australia in 1977–78, the then sixty-eight-year-old Don Bradman met the teams during a rest day at Adelaide. Bradman took the opportunity to face Aussie bowler Jeff Thomson, regarded by many as the fastest bowler of his generation. The Indian captain Bishan Singh Bedi said the sight was sheer magic. Bradman's positioning was impeccable even without any pads or gloves – 'or the damned box!'

'Thommo let one go on the leg and middle,' Bishan Singh Bedi said, 'and was promptly on-driven effortlessly.'

Bradman then told the bowler, 'This will teach you to have a mid-on for me, son!'

Thomson himself remarked, 'Why isn't this bastard playing with us tomorrow? That's how good I thought he was!'

In the 1975 Ashes series, Tony Greig selected Northamptonshire's David Steele although Steele was by then allegedly approaching retirement. Nevertheless, Greig considered the thirty-three-year-old as perhaps 'the most difficult player on the circuit to get out'.

When the silver-haired 'Stainless' Steele strode out to bat wearing a pair of steel-rimmed glasses, he was greeted with an assortment of comments from the Australians.

'Who the hell is this?' asked Dennis Lillee. Rod Marsh called over to Lillee, 'You didn't tell me your father was playing in this match.'

Jeff Thomson, meanwhile, remarked, 'Who've they picked now? Bloody Father Christmas?'

Steele did go on to provide a lovely present for the hitherto struggling England side. He hit nine fours, put on ninety-six for the fifth wicket with Greig before being dismissed for fifty and leaving to a standing ovation.

Talk show supremo and cricket lover Michael Parkinson said he once spoke to Harold Larwood about an encounter with Don Bradman. Bradman was, Larwood said, the greatest batsman to whom he ever bowled.

Larwood told how he had bowled to Bradman during the third Test of the 1930 Ashes. He thought the Australian had been caught out. Unfortunately the umpire did not agree and so Bradman got to bat on.

'Mind you,' said Larwood, 'we got him out shortly after.'

Parkinson asked how many runs Bradman had got in the meantime.

'Three hundred and thirty-four,' said Larwood.

Lancashire and England's George Duckworth's first trip to Australia in 1928 was also the last to include the great Jack Hobbs as a member of the team. Duckworth recalled that six years later, in 1934 when Hobbs was fifty-one, he came to play in a benefit match.

The weather was bitterly cold that day but nevertheless Hobbs hit the last first-class century of his career during the match. Afterwards he told Duckworth that he'd done it to try to get warm.

Richie Benaud once told Keith Miller, 'I wish I had been given the chance to bowl to Don Bradman. I came into the side just too late.'

'Richie, my boy,' Miller told him, 'your not having to bowl to Bradman was your one lucky break in cricket.'

English cricketer Wilfred Rhodes played the final day of his last Test match on 12 April 1930. He had been born in October 1877 and was therefore 52 years and 165 days old at the time of his final Test, making him the oldest cricketer to have played for England.

During his career, Rhodes played 1,110 first-class matches in which he bowled 185,742 balls, took 4,204 wickets and accumulated a tally of 39,969 runs. His other records include completing the double of 1,000 runs and 100 wickets in an English cricket season sixteen times. He made his first-class debut for Yorkshire aged twenty in May 1898 when Queen Victoria was still on the throne and lived until 1973, the year of the launch of Skylab, NASA's first space station.

Fred Titmus's playing career began in 1949 when he was sixteen. He was Middlesex's youngest ever player, and became a renowned off-spin bowler, winning a place in the England team from 1955.

He continued to play even after the horrific accident in 1968 in which he lost four toes to a motorboat propeller in the West Indies, and made his final appearance for Middlesex by accident in August 1982. On that occasion, the forty-nine-year-old Titmus had been attending a match against Surrey as a spectator when he was invited by Middlesex's captain Mike Brearley to play. Boots had to be found for him, but he went on to take 3 for 43 and helped Middlesex to victory.

In a pleasing symmetry, Titmus' 1949 debut had been alongside Brearley's father, Horace. Titmus had therefore played first-class cricket in five decades – from the 1940s to the 1980s. Although W. G. Grace had also achieved this level of longevity in the game, since the establishment of the County Championship in 1890 only Yorkshire's Wilfred Rhodes had matched this record.

Titmus was also one of just five first-class cricketers to have scored 20,000 runs and taken 2,500 wickets. The others were again Rhodes and Grace, as well as Yorkshire's George Hirst and Sussex's Maurice Tate.

Sachin Tendulkar wrote in his autobiography about how he and Shane Warne went to visit the legendary Don Bradman at his home in Adelaide in 1998.

Tendulkar asked Bradman how he thought he'd have coped if he were playing now and what he thought his Test average might be today.

'Around seventy probably,' said Bradman.

'Why seventy?' asked Tendulkar. 'Why not your actual average of ninety-nine?'

'Come on,' said Bradman, 'an average of seventy isn't bad for a ninety-year-old!'

In 1895, W. G. Grace made a return to form, which was particularly surprising as he was by this time aged fifty-one. He scored 2,346 runs, including nine centuries, which included the hundredth hundred of his career.

During a match between Gloucestershire and Sussex at Ashley Down Road, Bristol, Grace reached ninety-three and decided to declare. The reason for the decision was not to give Gloucestershire time to win the match. Instead it was because ninety-three was a score on which Grace had never finished any of the previous innings he had played. He just needed that one score entry of ninety-three to fill in the complete list of every number between zero and 100!

He wasn't just playing cricket; he was playing scorecard bingo!

But how would the great players of former, more civil times have responded to the verbal onslaughts and abuse received today? It just so happens that we know of at least one example of these two worlds colliding.

In February 1989, the then nearly eighty-year-old Don Bradman went to see Australia play the West Indics in Adelaide. Afterwards, Bradman met with the two teams in the West Indies dressing room and while most of the West Indian players greeted him, pacer Patrick Patterson accosted him, saying: 'You Don Bradman? You Don Bradman? I kill you, maan! I bowl at you, I kill you! I split you in two!'

There was a bit of an awkward silence for a moment until Bradman looked Patterson in the eye and told him: 'You couldn't even get Merv Hughes out! You'd have no chance against me, mate!'

TAILENDERS

And so our tour of *The Wicked Wit of Cricket* draws to a close but, even at this late stage, as the sun begins to dip over the pavilion roof, there's always a chance of a few last surprises from a motley collection of tailenders.

Cricketers famously like to take a direct approach. They are not ones to beat around the bush and would rather just tell it like it is. Or, to put it another way, their words can sometimes be as painful as a cricket ball pitched straight into the members' area.

After losing to Yorkshire at Bradford, Northamptonshire were out for revenge in the return match in July 1954. When Yorkshire's Johnny Wardle was bowled out for nought by Frank 'Typhoon' Tyson, Fred Trueman muttered at him, 'What a bloody stroke!' as he passed him on his way out to the crease.

Trueman, for his part, did not last much longer at the wicket. This gave Wardle the chance to get him back with a similar level of sarcasm: 'And a bloody fine shot that were, an' all!'

'Aye,' responded Trueman. 'I slipped on the pile of shit you dropped at the crease.'

During the 1932–33 bodyline Ashes series, the English captain Douglas Jardine overheard one member of the Australian team call him a bastard. Incensed by this, Jardine went to the Australian dressing room to demand an apology.

The Aussie vice-captain Vic Richardson answered the door and Jardine reported the matter. Richardson took in the seriousness of the issue before turning and yelling at his teammates: 'Okay, which of you bastards called this bastard "a bastard"?!'

During the bodyline series, England cricketer Patsy Hendren commented to his captain Douglas Jardine that the Australian fans 'don't really like you'.

'The feeling,' replied Jardine, 'is f***ing mutual!'

Fred Trueman once clean bowled a young batsman.

'That was a good ball, Fred,' commented the eager youngster.

'Aye,' said Trueman. 'And it were wasted on you.'

During a Sheffield Shield match, Steve Waugh was making lengthy preparations before facing his first ball.

Bowler Jamie Siddons finally lost patience and called to Waugh: 'For f***'s sake, mate! It's not a f***ing Test match!'

'I know it's not,' replied Waugh. 'You're here!'

During an Ashes Test in the 1960s, Fred Trueman was fielding near the gate to the pavilion. A new Aussie batsman coming out was about to shut the gate behind him when he heard Truman say: 'Don't bother shutting it, son, you won't be there long enough.'

During the final match of the 2006–07 Ashes in which England would suffer a 5–0 whitewash, one Australian commentator remarked: 'Well, Andrew Strauss is certainly an optimist – he's come out wearing sun block.'

Richie Benaud quipped, on noting Australian Glenn McGrath had achieved a not particularly impressive total when batting: 'And Glenn McGrath dismissed for two. Just ninety-eight runs short of his century.'

India's Ravi Shastri hit the ball towards Aussie twelfth man Mike Whitney, looking for a single.

'If you leave the crease,' Whitney told Shastri, 'I'll break your f***ing head!'

'If you could bat as well as you can talk,' replied Shastri, 'you wouldn't be the f***ing twelfth man!'

Indian cricket commentator Harsha Bhogle once remarked of spin bowler Narendra Hirwani: 'If you make a team of all the number-eleven batsmen in the world, Hirwani would still bat at number eleven!'

In a Test match at Port of Spain in Trinidad and Tobago, the third umpire Eddie Nicholls ruled West Indies cricketer Shivnarine Chanderpaul not out.

Former Indian cricketer Navjot Singh Sidhu was moved to comment that 'Eddie Nicholls is a man who cannot find his own buttocks with his two hands.'

Dennis Lillee once commented that Geoffrey Boycott was 'the only fellow I've met who fell in love with himself at a young age and has remained faithful ever since'.

It was announced that Geoffrey Boycott was going to be coaching the Pakistani team prior to their 2001 tour of England.

On hearing the news, Ian Botham commented: 'This can only help England's cause.'

When Ian Botham was awarded the England captaincy in May 1980, a sudden and dramatic loss of form seemed to follow. When he was relieved of the role a year later, he seemed to mystically regain his abilities once again.

Graham Dilley commented on Botham's rejuvenation that, 'It was almost as if you'd taken a child, made him an adult for a while, then allowed him to go back to being a child.'

Frances Edmonds, meanwhile, said of Botham that he was 'in no way inhibited by a capacity to over-intellectualize'.

Frances Edmonds also said of her husband Phil: 'He's got a reputation for being awkward and arrogant, probably because he is awkward and arrogant.'

And Mrs Edmonds also described David Gower as follows: 'It's difficult being more laid-back than David Gower without actually being comatose.'

David Lloyd commented when he first saw New Zealand cricketer Nathan Astle: 'If this bloke's a Test-match bowler, then my backside is a fire engine.'

While working in the commentary box, Ian Chappell made the following observation about Phil Tufnell: 'The other advantage England have when Tufnell is bowling is that he isn't fielding.'

On seeing a player drop a catch, Geoffrey Boycott commented: 'I reckon my mum could have caught that in her pinny!'

And on seeing another dropped catch, Boycott said: 'He could have caught that between the cheeks of his backside!'

Former player Ray East once summed up his current level of abilities: 'I can't bat, can't bowl and can't field these days. I've every chance of being picked for England.'

Martin Johnson once gave his assessment of Graeme Hick: 'At least we are safe from an intoxicating rendition of "There's only one Graeme Hick". There are, quite clearly, two of them. The first one turns out for teams like Worcestershire and New Zealand's Northern Districts and plays like a god. The second one pulls on an England cap and plays like an anagram of god.'

Johnson also said of Michael Atherton that he was 'one of the few people capable of looking more dishevelled at the start of a six-hour century than at the end of it'.

And of Kevin Pietersen, Johnson wrote, 'It would be a surprise if the mirrors in Pietersen's house totalled anything less than the entire stock at one of the larger branches of B&Q.'

Steve Waugh once instructed Ricky Ponting to field under Nasser Hussain's nose. Ian Healy responded: 'That could be anywhere inside a three-mile radius!'

The sportswriter Rick Broadbent commented of Merv Hughes that he 'always appeared to be wearing a tumble-dried ferret on his top lip'.

On another occasion, Broadbent summed up Kevin Pietersen: 'He is big and brash and as subtle as colonic irrigation.'

In 1994, during a warm-up match between England and an ACB Chairman's XI, Dennis Lillee was faced by the slightly less-than-slim Mike Gatting.

'Move out the way, Gatt,' Lillee called to him. 'I can't see the stumps.'

Keith Miller was perhaps Australia's greatest ever all-rounder, but his cricketing career was rudely interrupted by the Second World War. During the war, Miller joined the Royal Australian Air Force. He was eventually assigned to 169 Squadron at Great Massingham in Norfolk, from where he took part in missions into France and Germany in April and May 1945.

On one occasion, one of the bombs he was carrying failed to release and was left dangling from his plane. Miller then had to return to England still with the bomb hanging from one wing and land without blowing himself up.

Later in life, Michael Parkinson asked him about the pressure he felt playing in Test matches.

'Pressure?' scoffed Miller. 'There's no pressure in Test cricket. Real pressure is when you are flying a Mosquito with a Messerschmitt up your arse!'